DEAN SWIFT

From the painting by Charles Jervas.

Reproduced by kind permission of the Board of Governors and Guardians of the National Gallery of Ireland.

SWIFT
AND HIS CIRCLE

A Book of Essays

BY

R. WYSE JACKSON

With a Foreword by

SEUMAS O'SULLIVAN

THE TALBOT PRESS LIMITED
DUBLIN

First published 1945

Printed at The Talbot Press, Dublin

To

N O L A

The author is indebted to *The Dublin Magazine*, *The Irish Times*, *The Irish Press*, Radio Eireann, and the *Irish Digest* for their kind permission to reproduce a number of these essays.

FOREWORD

Dr. Wyse Jackson has asked me to write a brief foreword to his collection of Swiftiana, but even if I were competent to write on a subject which he has made so peculiarly his own, the author of *Jonathan Swift Dean and Pastor* needs no introduction to anyone who is a student of the greatest of 18th century writers. When that small but important book was published in 1939, it was hailed at once by competent critics as one of the clearest, most acute and convincing solutions of certain problems which have baffled many of Swift's biographers, from Orrery to Quintana. But the very ease with which Dr. Jackson has confronted and elucidated those vexed problems which have made the work of the earlier biographers and critics so unsatisfactory to those who have realised, as Sir Henry Craik has so well written, " how keenly sensitive was the heart buried under all that weight of misanthropy and cynicism; how much his pride was rooted in earnestness, his anger in hatred of oppression," the very clarity and brevity with which he achieved his purpose, may blind at least " the common reader " to the vast amount of research, the loving and unsparing labour which are involved in such a task.

In this collection of essays we get at least some idea of those many by-paths which he has explored on the way to his triumphant journey's end. Here we are confronted by no mere assemblage of biographical, bibliographical details; in these pages we are brought into contact with no mere collection of resurrected ghosts. Rather we find ourselves amongst the living, breathing personalities who made up that circle in which Swift lived—and reigned. Stella, that " little mother " for a man who in spite of all his brilliance and fame, was rather lonely and pathetically in need of " mothering " ; Vanessa, " unhappy young woman " as she styles herself towards the close of her tragic life; " Dear brainless Dingley," whom Alice Meynell has bravely championed, " No one else in literary history has been so defrauded of her honours " ; Roger, Parish Clerk of Laracor, that " grey-coated, red-waistcoated little rascal " who was, incidentally, a writer of excellent occasional verse; he must have, as I have often thought, resembled another Parish Clerk, of whom we read in the notes to Southey's Life of Wesley, but Roger was a much better poet than the author of the lines quoted by Southey :

> " *King William has come home again,*
> *King William home has come,*"

and he deserves to be remembered, were it only for those three lines :

> " The Doctor smiled upon them both;
> I love to see the Doctor smile,
> For it's the sunshine of our isle."

Sprightly little Letitia Pilkington, of whom we are told that " the Dean watched her literary freaks much as a mastiff might watch the gambols of a kitten," and whose pretty face has been immortalized in a magnificent mezzotint by Purcell, after a painting by Nathaniel Hone; Mrs. Barber, to whom Swift showed much kindness, and of whom he wrote that rather caustic recommendation (to The Earl of Orrery) : " She hath one qualification that I wish all good poets posses'd a share of : I mean that she is ready to take advice, and have her verses corrected by those who are generally allowed to be the best judges " ; that amazing young scholar, Mrs. Grierson, who died at the age of 27, but " had managed to become a perfect adept in Hebrew, Greek, Latin, Mathematics, History and Divinity " ; Mrs. Sican, of whom one would like to hear more, for we have on record the fact that she sent the Dean " a birthday Royal Sturgeon, and a present of Spanish Liquorice " ; the gentle poet, Parnell, of whom Swift wrote, " He passeth all the poets of the day by a bar's length," and for whom he had a genuine affection.

All of these, and many others, live and move and have their being again in these charming essays. But " I intend not a volume of praises larger than his book," and I will no longer obtrude myself between Dr. Jackson and the readers of a volume from which I have derived so much pleasure—and instruction.

SEUMAS O'SULLIVAN.

CONTENTS

Swift loved mankind, but loathed
The flesh that clothed
Humanity. Scorn that was pain, and pity shorn
Of tenderness he felt,
And stoutly dealt
Harsh blows for those he sheltered with his loving scorn.

Still lives the Intellect
We dare dissect
With Lilliputian skill. We cannot kill that breath:
It sears. We probe, distraught,
Each secret thought
Of one poor lacerated heart unhealed by death.

—NOLA JACKSON.

SWIFT AND HIS CIRCLE.

" THE REVEREND DOCTOR JONATHAN SWIFT, Late Dean of St. Patrick's, deceased October the 19th, 1745, and was interred the 22nd of the same, at the second pillar from the west gate in the south side of the great aisle . . ."

(*Register of St. Patrick's Cathedral*).

*   *   *

SOMEONE cut off a lock of his hair with a scissors on the day he lay in state, two hundred years ago. In his desk, long forgotten by him was a dusty wisp of dark, greying hair. " Only a woman's hair " he had written long ago in his crabbed, meticulous handwriting. And now someone had stolen a wisp from his own frosted, baffled death's head.

" Only a Struldbrug's hair " they might have entitled it. The hair of a great man who had outlived everything; friends, reason, usefulness; but who did not die until a generation past his time.

Swift lay in his coffin that October evening in 1745. For days his shabby, pale-faced people filed past him to pay him tribute. They have been marching past ever since, for Swift left something that did not die. He left a passionate

will for justice which lived through two centuries.
The great epitaph lives. It is scored deep into
the black stone—and it links everything of
citizenship and courage we possess with the
tortured Prometheus of St. Patrick's Close.

> *HERE lies the body of Jonathan Swift*
> *Where rage and resentment can*
> *No longer*
> *Eat into the heart.*
> *Go, passer by,*
> *And do, if you can, as he did,—*
> *A man's part*
> *In the defence of liberty.*

An agonised satirist of the twentieth century
walked through fetid slums where rags hung out
on clothes lines beside the ironical golden balls
of mean pawnshops, and snarled :

"The government plan for starving the destitute to death has had a serious check. A scientist
has discovered that there is enough vitamin H in
a boiled banana skin to keep a family of six alive
for two days. The Ministry of Health goes
further and says that, by making an effort, a
family of six could be kept going for four days."

Two centuries earlier Swift's acid pen etched
out the same frenzied protest for the down and
out. He used the obscene force of his savage
irony against the heartlessness of the administra-

tion in his *Modest Proposal*—a scheme for eating peasant children as the least miserable way out of life.

" I grant this food will be somewhat dear, and therefore very proper for landlords, who, as they have already devoured most of the parents; seem to have the best title to the children."

Maybe he hated mankind. He said that he did; he confessed that the piled-up selfishness of men tortured his spirit past endurance. But he loved Tom, Dick and Harry, and it is in this setting of fellowship we would show him. He had friends, and if we would understand him aright we should do well to see him in his Irish circle, with those whose personality made contact with his. " Fellowship is Heaven; lack of Fellowship is Hell," cried the preacher, and there were some whose fellowship brought happiness to a very suffering man. His patron, Sir William Temple, had once written, that " the greatest Medicine is a true Friend." We would remember those who were Jonathan Swift's true friends.

In 1713 he had come to Dublin. He believed it was to be his Siberia—the trap for a poisoned rat. Truth to tell, it came to be his spiritual home and the place where he came nearest to true living. Dublin gave him his usefulness and his immortality—Dublin which created the Dean, the Drapier and Gulliver.

Ireland served Swift well in his friends. He had left behind him Pope and Arbuthnot and Gay. He found in their place a circle which gave him affection and loyalty—that Irish companionability which he needed, and one is glad that he came to realise it soon enough.

> " The difference is not much between
> St. James' Park and Stephen's Green;
> And Dawson Street will serve as well
> To lead you thither as Pall Mall. . . .
>
> The Dean and Sheridan, I hope
> Will half supply a Gay and Pope.
> Corbet, though yet I know his worth not,
> No doubt will prove a good Arbuthnot.
> What think you of my favourite clan,
> Robin and Jack, and Jack and Dan;
> Fellows of modest worth and parts,
> With cheerful looks and honest hearts ? "

It was a pleasant circle. There was Thomas Sheridan, that " creature without cunning," who played David to Swift's Saul. His contribution was purely unselfish, for he was the worst man in the world for his own interests. It *would* be Sheridan to lose his first decent preferment for preaching in sheer inadvertence from the text " Sufficient unto the day is the evil thereof " on the King's birthday. " What business had you," enquired Swift, " to speak of a halter in a family

where one of it was hanged ? " But he gave
Swift the devotion he needed so badly, and he
was a loyal companion until the demon of madness made companionship no longer possible,
and a pathetic break in the friendship came a
few months before his death.

There was Parson Dan Jackson with the funny
nose, much satirised, and his brother, Parson
Jack, of Santry, who lived to inherit Swift's
furniture and third best beaver hat. There were
the clerical Grattans, Robert and John; James
Corbet, too, Stella's executor and a subsequent
Dean of St. Patrick's; and Patrick Delaney,
who married Mrs. Pendarves, Mary Granville.
For years " D.D."—Dr. Delaney—was Swift's
Chapter colleague, and he was the author of that
kindly and authoritative biography—*Observations
on Lord Orrery's Remarks*—which appeared in
1754. It was a happy circle. There was Pre-
bendary Worrall, whose *table d'hote* dinners
Swift enjoyed; Archdeacon Walls of the little
ombre and conversation club; Physician Richard
Helsham, whose gift of humour ministered to
his ill-health.

> " And then if friend Dick will but ope your
>   back door, he
>   Will quickly dispel the black clouds that
>   hang o'er ye."

There were old friends like Charles Ford, of Wood Park in Meath, and new ones like William Dunkin, the poet, and Faulkner, the Prince of Printers, who placed the bust of Swift in St. Patrick's to flank the flaming epitaph.

Swift has often been accused of pulling strings for ecclesiastical preferment. So he did—but in almost every case they were pulled for the benefit of his friends. And if we are to judge by that delightful eighteenth century epitaph of the worthy Mrs. Bate, the art of " using influence " was not yet counted as improper.

> " *Here rests all that was mortal of Mrs. Elizabeth Bate*
>> *A Woman of unaffected Piety*
>> *And exemplary Virtue.*
>>
>> *She was honourably descended*
>> *And by means of her Alliance to*
>> *The Illustrious Family of Stanhope*
>> *She had the merit to obtain*
>> *For her husband and children*
>> *Twelve separate employments*
>> *In Church and State.*
>
> *She died June 7; 1751, in the 75th year of her age.*"

Swift had no qualms about looking for employment. But give him this credit—it was for his companions he got livings, not himself. He served his friends well.

If he had the art of writing the utterly damning testimonial—" Whereas the bearer served me the space of one year, during which time he was an idler and a drunkard, I then discharged him as such; but how far his having been five years at sea may have mended his manners I leave to the penetration of those who may hereafter choose to employ him "—Swift could also charm those in power with the most lyrical epistles on behalf of people he liked. He was sincere in his friendships and we should believe him when he gives his motive for writing to Lord Carteret about poor Sheridan.

" I hope you will please to believe that this request proceeds wholly from justice and humanity; for he is neither a dependent nor a relation of mine."

*　　　*　　　*

They were many, these friends. Some are forgotten; some have been recalled in these pages. Round Swift circles an Irish cavalcade, gravitating to him by the magnetism of his personality. Roger, the Clerk of Laracor; gentle, raven-haired Stella; dear, comfortable, brainless Mrs. Dingley; Cousin Martha Whiteway, loyal to the last; forthright Mrs. Brent, that sturdy

Presbyterian housekeeper who ran his tradesmen's lending bank for him; sly gossiping little Mrs. Pilkington and the other three Dublin poetesses; cheering cap-waving weavers of the Liberties; learned Doctors of the College; the seraglio of violet and plum and hob-nail sellers; bishops; beggars; workmen; housewives. Think of them kindly, these Dublin ghosts who were friends of Jonathan Swift.

"LOOK—HERE COMES DEAN SWIFT!"

HAZLITT has a thrilling essay in which he makes a group of people discuss the great figures whom they would like to recall. It concludes with a sentence which must be ranked among the noblest of literature :

" If Shakespeare was to come into the room, we should all rise up to meet him; but if that person was to come into it, we should all fall down and try to kiss the hem of his garment."

It would be the most glorious of privileges to meet the saints, the heroes, the geniuses, the patriots of the past.

And for the Dubliners, the place and the time and the person would very likely be—the outskirts of Dublin, on, say, the 27th of October, 1724, and going to see Jonathan Swift, the Drapier.

We should probably be only too glad to pass quickly through the rural districts around the city. We should see things evil enough to leave an ugly taste in the mouth. Out in God's sunshine, filthy rickety children grubbing among dug-out potato drills for the remnants of food. Thatched mud and straw hovels, from which issues a horrible miasma of dirt and damp. Emaciated slatterns, beggars in rags. We begin to understand how Swift could write :—

"I confess myself to be touched with a very sensitive pleasure when I hear of a mortality in any country parish or village, where the wretches are forced to pay for a filthy cabin and two ridges of potatoes, treble their worth; brought up to steal or beg for want of work; to whom death would be the best thing to be wished for on account both of themselves and of the public." We begin to realise why it is that Swift has his crazy, mad fanaticism for justice, and why he tells of the agonised laceration of his heart by savage indignation. As we jog along the suburbs of the city we begin to agree heartily with the metaphysical George Berkeley that quite certainly there is nowhere "so beggarly, wretched and destitute a people" as the unfortunate Irish.

The day being what it is—October 27th—we see here and there about the city a notice, read with amused interest by little knots of tradesmen, who smile knowingly at one another. It offers £300 reward "to such person or persons as shall within the specified six months from the date hereof, discover the author of the said pamphlet, so that he be apprehended and convicted thereby."

Quite certainly some of the group will show us the pamphlet—the fourth *Letter to the Whole People of Ireland*, still hot from the Press—and tell us that any officials who venture to molest or arrest Dean Swift will inevitably be lynched out of hand and with great pleasure by the good citizens of Dublin.

By now our interest is kindled sufficiently to make us spur our horse into a canter as we head towards the thickly-populated part of the old city where Swift lives, and where Minot's great tower (still without the embellishment of a spire) stands out as a landmark above the Liberty of the Dean of St. Patrick's.

We find ourselves in a network of narrow streets—streets where we meet a formidable variety of effluvia, for nobody yet cares much about sanitation. Streets and houses—houses of wattle-and-daub, half-timbered houses of the old century; ingeniously variegated gabling in the Dutch fashion; a few brand-new houses in the cold " Palladian " style—red brick and severely classical limestone porticos—all grouped around Comyn's great Early English church of St. Patrick. Through the windows of some of the upper rooms we see here and there a handloom, for in this district the weavers dwell. The narrow and not too clean streets are crowded. A forest of shop signs creak over our heads.

Dozens of poky little drapers' shops try to make us stop and buy " arras, baize, bewpers, bombazaines, bus-yarns, blankets, callamancoes, carrells, chamblettes, dormicks, durance, damasks," and half a hundred other kinds of quaintly-named cloths.

We arrive at the Cathedral, doubtful of what we are going to expect. Shall we like him, or shall we hate him ? Swift's personality admits of no shades of approval: either we shall love him or detest him, and he may either be very kind to us, or abominably rude. We remember apprehensively how he made a " paltry curate " drink down the dregs of claret as penance for bumptiousness, and how George Faulkner, twitted for being so weak-minded as to eat asparagus-stalks when Swift ordered him to, complained with feeling : " If he bid *you* eat *your* stalks, you would have done it, too ! "

It is a lucky moment. We see him just as he is coming out of the Cathedral after morning prayer (he goes every morning when his head does not ache too much). He is an upright, middle-aged figure, coming close to sixty years of age. Harsh lines of pain have furrowed a face which was full of life and quickness, but which now is growing heavy and a little dead. Somehow we get the impression that his smile is rather wry, a little twisted, as if one side of his face is slightly paralysed.

But where is the terrible ogre of whom we had heard ? That black-clad elderly man with the buckled shoes and the attendant beadle is cracking jokes with a bunch of poor old ladies—surely the quaintest collection of pathetic oddities Dublin can produce ! We begin to suspect that the ferocious Swift is a legend—where does that benevolent old gentleman fit in ? Then suddenly the black brows come together and the pleasant twisted smile vanishes, and gives place to a snarl. We see him glaring with a startling intensity of hatred at the filthy hand which a vermin-infested beggarwoman is holding out.

We hear the high-pitched rather nasal and grating voice rap out : " Water is not so dear but that you could wash. Nothing for you while your hands are dirty." The little incident seems revealing of the character of the man. Then the morning levee ends. We see him now proceeding through the huddle of beggars whom he has helped to that gloomy bachelor-house, the Deanery.

Perhaps we will not risk knocking at that door after all. We have our doubts whether he will suffer gladly fools or journalists or tourists from two centuries ahead in time. But we will talk to this intelligent-eyed little artisan who is standing beside us. We notice his blackened labourer's hands and his frayed and rusty black coat and knee-breeches—but more than that, we notice the curious light of enthusiasm which seems to glow in his face as he follows the Dean with his eyes until the Deanery door slams to.

"Yes," he tells us. "He is the friend of all the poor people like myself who work here in the Liberty. We all know about his charity, and many of us have reason to thank him for it. Personally, he lent me money to set up in my own business. My cousin, who is one of his footmen, says that he gives away one-third of his income, no less. Just to give you an idea of what he will do, let me tell you how he arrived home last week on foot and out of breath, having hurried to escape a shower. When he came in to the hall he gave sixpence to my cousin. ' I have saved this on car hire,' said our Dean. ' Go and give it instead to that old man at the corner who sells gingerbread '."

"Very interesting," we say. "But we have not got long to wait here, and so, while we have time, do tell us something about his work as the Drapier."

The little rusty-coated man's eyes light up. And this is the story that he has to tell—the story of how Swift, under the pseudonym of

" The Drapier," fought the state project to foist a copper coinage upon Ireland.

The Duchess of Kendal, who was the King's mistress, and who had a pension on the Irish establishment of £3,000 per annum, had wheedled out of his Majesty the patent for a supply of copper coins for Ireland. This she traded with one William Wood, a Birmingham hardware manufacturer, for the sum of £10,000. His instructions were to make coins valued at £100,800 out of £60,000 worth of metal. From the remaining £40,800 Wood agreed to pay £10,000 to the Duchess and £14,000 to the Crown, retaining £16,800 as his share of the bargain.

That was the plan—but Swift's brilliant pen smashed the whole scheme. His pamphlets and verses, cunningly written in a pseudo-simple and honest style, roused the man in the street into a frenzy of panic-stricken opposition. At last the project had to be dropped, and the Government paid Wood £24,000 for abandoning his patent.

Consider one or two examples of the Drapier's technique. •Dealing with the supposedly debased nature of Wood's halfpence, he says : " If a squire has a mind to come to town to buy clothes and wines and spices for himself and family, or perhaps to pass the winter here, he must bring with him five or six horses well laden with sacks, as the farmers bring their corn; and when his lady comes in her coach to the shops it must be followed with a car loaded with Mr. Wood's money."

Again, in the second Drapier letter, he appeals to the avariciousness of the man in the street by means of some entirely fallacious—but how effective—statistics :

" Shopkeepers, look to yourselves ! Wood will oblige and force you to take 5½d. of his trash in every payment; and many of you receive twenty, thirty, forty payments in one day, or else you can hardly find bread. And pray consider how much that will amount to in a year. Twenty times 5½d. is 9s. 2d.; wherein you will be losers of at least £140 by taking your payment in Wood's money."

Yes—Swift was a master of the modern art of propaganda; that people will swallow anything that they really want to believe ! The Government, as we have seen, did not appreciate the joke, but no informer could be found against Swift. Yet everyone knew his responsibility, and when Walpole spoke of arresting him he was told that his police would need a guard of ten thousand soldiers in order to do it. The people received Swift as their champion, and when he returned to town in 1726 after the cause had been won, he was met by all Dublin and escorted home in triumph amid the pealing of church bells and the blaze of bonfires. Towns voted him their freedom—for instance, he became a Freeman both of Dublin and of Cork.

It was a triumphant agitation—and one cannot think of any other writer in English literature who could have brought it off so effectively. Yes !—after all we decide that we must speak to the Drapier, even at the risk of a snub. We climb the steps to the heavy panelled door and lift the great brass knocker . . .

THE DRAPIER AND THE THEATRE

THAT curious Limerick character, Dan Hayes, who wrote his own charming epitaph " *Dan Hayes, an honest man and a lover of his country,*" was once credited with the authorship of "Hamlet." So a Kilkenny playbill states.

"KILKENNY THEATRE ROYAL
By His Majesty' Company of
Comedians
(The Last Night, because the Company
go to-morrow to Waterford)
On Saturday, May 4, 1793,
Will be performed, by Command of
Several Respectable Persons
in this learned metropolis,
for the benefit of MR. KEARNS
THE TRAGEDY OF HAMLET
Originally written and composed by
the celebrated
Dan Hayes of Limerick, and inserted in
Shakespeare's Works.
Hamlet by Mr. Kearns (being his first
appearance in this character) who between
the acts will perform several solos on the

patent bagpipes, which play two tunes at the same time. Ophelia, by Mrs. Prior, will introduce several favourite airs in character, particularly ' The Lass of Richmond Hill ' and ' We'll all be happy together ' from the Rev. Mr. Dibdin's Oddities."

Yes—even that could happen in the fantastic Irish eighteenth century theatre ! It was shockingly bad in spite of the twinkling of occasional stars like Peg Woffington, Foote, Barry and that pompous, heartless ass, Mossop, or the rare appearance of a Sheridan.

It is significant of the worthlessness of the stage of the day that Swift ignored it. He tried most forms of art, from cantata to Pindaric odes ; epigrams, biography, history and fiction ; but he did not write for the stage. Apart from giving a youthful kick at "The Stage Itinerant," and advising his fellow-clergy to see " The Beggars' Opera," he snubbed the theatre by leaving it severely alone.

There is just one exception. On one occasion Swift contributed a trifle of verse to a play. A fragment which links up with his battle for the survival of the Dublin woollen trade.

Our present poplin firms are in the tradition of that great textile industry which lived in the heart of old Dublin. The woollen trade then was the livelihood of thousands of men and women congregated in the Liberties. In 1721, even after repressive measures against the industry had been clamped on for years, there were still seventeen hundred Dublin men dependent on the weaving business, together with their wives and families. It is amazing that so many survived, for in 1699 the Irish had been prohibited from exporting their wares to any country whatsoever. It was a fantastically oppressive law. As Swift wrote : " Ireland is the only kingdom I ever heard or read of, either in ancient or modern history, which was denied the liberty of exporting their native commodities and manufactures wherever they pleased, except to countries at war with their own prince and state."

At one blow world markets had been blockaded, All that was left was the small home demand. And here comes the occasion of Swift's one excursion into theatrical writing, when a play was produced for the benefit of the starving weavers. Sheridan wrote the prologue, and the Dean an epilogue which versified his thunderings on behalf of home industries.

" We'll dress in manufactures made at home;
Equip our kings and gen'rals at the Comb.
We'll rig in Meath Street Egypt's haughty queen,

And Antony shall court her in ratteen.
In blue shallon shall Hannibal be clad,
And Scipio trail an Irish purple plad."

The condition of those Dublin weavers was deplorable. Gradually looms, tools and furniture were sold off for bread by the dwindling survivors, and when starvation level had long been reached a church collection and a grant of one hundred pounds was officially ordered for the benefit of the six thousand victims of the strangled industry ! Swift's work for the life of the trade is worth recognising. His dramatic excursion was neither the beginning nor the end of what he attempted. He bearded his archbishop with an ultimatum that the clergy should wear Dublin-made black gowns. He laid out five hundred pounds of private capital, without possibility of profit, on loan to Dublin tradesmen. And he focused public opinion once for all in his hard-hitting " *Proposal for a Universal Use of Irish Manufactures.*"

It was a failure of course. One victory like that of the Wood's Halfpence is about all that the most persevering fighter can reasonably expect. Still, he made the effort—and it deserves honour. If Boyle was Father of Chemistry and Brother of the Earl of Cork, Swift was most certainly the Father of Home Industry—and Brother of Sean and Seumas of the Coombe.

ROGER COX, SWIFT'S FACTOTUM.

THE POETICAL PARISH CLERK OF LARACOR.

AROUND planets of the larger kind we find satellites revolving. It is the same with great men. We cannot think of Don Quixote without his Sancho Panza or of Dr. Johnson without James Boswell. Mr. Pickwick would somehow be incomplete if he did not have in tow his Cockney sparrow, Sam Weller. Sherlock Holmes would be quite inconceivable without the proximity of Dr. Watson. And for the completeness of our Irish legendary Dean Swift it is pleasant to think of his foil—Roger Cox, the Parish Clerk of Laracor.

Laracor in County Meath was the toy parish of Dean Swift for some fifty and more years. In the hurly-burly of high politics and during the years of his struggle for the Irish man-in-the-street, Laracor was Swift's retreat. But Laracor would not have been complete without Roger— that quaint figure with a red waistcoat who shadowed his master and reflected something of his master's native wit.

Roger belongs to a vanished race. He was a

parish clerk—a member of that very minor religious order who led the singing in the parishes of the Established Church of a century or so ago, and answered the responses for the congregation at the proper places. They usually bore the generic nickname of " Old Amen," and they had a humble reading desk below the pulpit from which to say it. Their work was thoroughly miscellaneous. As often as not, they taught the youth of the parish. They rang church bells. They were by way of being village oracles. A typical member of the order is described by Sir Jonah Barrington. He was the perfect jack of all trades—surveyor, farrier, cattle doctor, bone-setter. " He was also a famous brewer and accountant—in fine, was everything at Cullenagh —steward, agent, caterer, farmer, sportsman, secretary, clerk to the colonel as a magistrate, and also clerk to Mr. Barrat as the parson; but he would not sing a stave in church, though he'd chant indefatigably in the hall. . . . He had a turning lathe, a number of grindstones, and a carpenter's bench in his room. He used to tin the sauce pans, which act he called *chymistry;* and I have seen him like a tailor, putting a new cape to his riding coat ! He made all sorts of nets, and knit stockings; but, above all, he piqued himself on the variety and depth of his *learning.*"

Roger Cox, Parish Clerk of Laracor, was the

life and soul of every wake and wedding around County Meath. Being a jovial soul, he received an automatic invitation to every rustic festivity for miles around Trim. His respectability was sometimes marred by rather too much conviviality —but he must have been a lovable soul.

The best-known anecdote which survives about him is that legend first told by Lord Orrery in 1752, of how he shared in a week-day service in Laracor church with Jonathan Swift—not then Dublin's Dean, but a very humble vicar.

It was on a Wednesday—and Swift's fifteen "gentle, simple" parishioners were, unfortunately, too busy to remember to come to Parson Swift's service. But Roger, of course, was there as clerk. The hour of service came and went. And still the congregation failed to appear. At last Swift started the service, startlingly modifying the traditional opening words of Morning Prayer to "Dearly Beloved Roger, the scripture moveth you and me," etc. !

The modern Church of Ireland has entirely forgotten this curious race of ecclesiastical dignitaries, the parish clerks. But they survived well into the last century, and as an order they contained many "Characters." There is a delightful article about these functionaries in the rare "College Magazine" of Dublin University for 1857. One would have liked to have met the hero of that article, one Joe Bralligan, who combined the trades of butcher and blue-dyer with freelance preaching, bell-ringing and psalmsinging in Sunday church. Joe, in tow wig and white cravat had a mighty voice and a " compass of about three-quarters of the octave."

("In church none ever heard a layman
With a clearer voice say ' Amen,'
Who now with Hallelujah's sound
Like him can make the roofs rebound ? ")

It was Joe who made a devastating reply to a curate who ventured to hint that his powerful voice drowned the rest of the congregation.

"My dear child, I see you don't yet know my place ; to be sure I drown them ! Why, if I didn't, they would all be out of tune and our music would not be worth listening to."

Another of the same class was that "Mr. Wimpe, Clerk of Parish " at Carrick-on-Suir, of whom Dorothea Herbert records in her " Retrospections " that he was her writing, reading, and grammar master, and the family's " Prime Minister " on all occasions.

Now, the convivial Parish Clerk of Laracor is of interest for other reasons beyond his association with Jonathan Swift. He deserves to be featured as a versifier in his own right, inasmuch as he was inspired by Swift to a considerable output of verse in the manner of Samuel Butler. It is said that Swift himself could repeat all " Hudibras " by heart. In Roger, the Dean had a fervent disciple and imitator—perhaps the first of a host of Irish followers. Apart from an extract from one poem quoted elsewhere by the writer, none of Roger's verses seem yet to have appeared in print.

The most interesting of his works is an account of a wedding at Laracor. It is said to have been written in the Marriage Register of the parish. (It was Roger's business to keep the records). Significantly it begins with the line : " Sam Butler was a man of wit." This poem goes on to give the conventional advice of Mr. Punch to those about to marry. But the poet does know at least one happy exception.

> " 'Twas I am sure on Monday last
>   That Kate and Ned were tied so fast
>   That Time himself, tho' he should try it
>   I'm very sure will ne'er untie it,
>   And Death will scarce dissolve the bands
>   That bind such mutual hearts and hands."

An allusion to the officiating minister follows :

> " They both were tied by Dr. Swift,
>   And Kate had put on her best shift,
>   With cap and handkerchief as white
>   As snow on a December night."

Twenty-eight lines of highly sentimental thoughts about the bridal pair follow. Then come at the close three extremely interesting lines :

" The Doctor smiled upon you both;
I love to see the Doctor smile,
For it's the sunshine of our isle."

Probably the happiest time in Swift's troubled life was that short period when his chief interest was in landscape gardening at Laracor and in looking after the tiny congregation of his queer little parish church. In these three lines we see a reflection of those days.

In another unpublished poem entitled " The Landlord," Roger Cox presents a dialogue between two peasants. The questioner is asking the reason for his friend's hang-dog air :

" Dear Pat of late you seem so sad;
The times I know are very bad ;
Take courage, man, they can't be worse.
I wouldn't give a single curse
For one that lets his spirits sink
When he can eat and sleep and drink.
For different wounds we've different salves;
You've still three cows and they have calves;
You have a mare as black as jet;
You have one lamb, and that's a pet;

You have some barley in your barn,
And three good webs of homespun yarn;
You have a suit of cloaths for Sunday,
And you'll begin to plough on Monday;
Your family are all in health—
Why, Pat, you wallow in your wealth.
Then tell me, why of late so sad ?
I know the times are very bad,
But when they're at the worst they'll mend,
Speak out, you know that I'm your friend ! "

The cheery optimism is quite in character with what local traditions recall of Roger's easy care-free spirit. But Pat's reply recalls the deplorable social conditions of the day :

" You see that house on yonder hill ?
I swear then by St. Columbkill,
Long as that house is in my sight
I cannot rest by day or night.
My landlord riots 'neath its roof,
His heart is steel'd, it's musket proof;
In manners he's a perfect bruin;
His whole delight his tenant's ruin.
The widow's tears can't quench his thirst;
Of all men breathing he's the worst.
Long as that house is in my sight
I cannot rest there day or night
It brings to mind the half-year's day;
The cash, or all is swept away."

Another sentimental fragment—in which the influence of Swift is less apparent—describes in luscious terms a deserted maiden.

> " Her lip a cherry bathed in dew;
> Her cheeks, I can't describe their hue,
> For e'en the rose-bud will not do;
> Her hair, the dawn of orient skies;
> And then again her sloe-black eyes,
> Enough to set a saint on fire,
> What more could mortal man desire ? "

" Interest Like Rust," the last set of verses surviving, lament the unexpected way in which a long loan of ten pounds accumulates a huge burden of interest. The concluding lines, containing as they do a passing comment on Swift's preaching, will be sufficient to quote as a final sample of the works of this pleasant little companion of Swift's country life.

> " So sure as Swift sticks to his text,
> So sure I'll pay you Monday next.
> I kept my word and brought the cash,
> And as I thought to cut a dash
> Put twenty guineas in my purse
> Long hoarded up by my good nurse.
> Tim handed me a long account,
> But can you guess the whole amount ?
> Why then, to save you all the trouble,
> The whole I swear was nearly double.

At first in truth it struck me dumb;
I found it right and paid the sum.
Henceforward let it not be told,
By young, by middle-aged or old
That purest gold is free from rust.
No ! Interest is a canker'd crust
That preys on gold and precious stones,
As some disease preys on the bones."

*　　　　*　　　　*

They were the closest of friends—this vicar of Laracor and his Sancho Panza. They coincided admirably in politics and in temperament and in humour. They were an ideal parochial team. As Roger punningly describes the relationship, " although they said words about " (in church at the service) " yet they never disagreed."

The last glimpse of this grey-coated, red-waistcoated little rascal is pure comedy.

Swift had set Roger down to dine off a very-much-carved hambone. (The Dean, one remembers, was notoriously careful of the pennies.) Roger protested that the bone had nothing on it worth eating. " Sirrah, rogue," said Swift in mock rage, " do you not know that the nearer the bone the sweeter the meat ? "

That afternoon they were out riding. At the end of the journey Roger tethered Swift's horse to a large and very bare boulder.

" What do you mean, rascal ? " exploded Swift.

" Do you not know, master," retorted Roger with a face of sweet innocence, " that the nearer the rock, the sweeter the grass ? "

And here we bid adieu to Roger Cox.

SWIFT, STELLA AND VANESSA.

DID SWIFT MARRY STELLA ?

THE moment anyone mentions Dean Swift, the question immediately crops up : " What about Stella ? Did he marry her or did he not ? "

Everyone asks that question, and the answer usually is vague, like that given not so long ago by an old lady living in Stella's cottage near Trim : " Some says she was his wife, and some says she wasn't, but whatever she was, she was something to him."

So far, so good, but rather indefinite ! But, fortunately, there is evidence which can make us commit ourselves further and say with conviction : " Yes, it is our firm belief that she was his wife."

*　　　　*　　　　*

The curtain rises on the first act of the drama in the year 1689. We see the prim shorn lawns of a great garden opening up a vista towards Sir William Temple's vast mansion at Moor Park. We peep through the lattice window into a schoolroom. A saturnine, fierce-eyed young man sits there. He is shabby and lonely—a penniless exile from Dublin eking out an existence as secretary to Sir William.

Esther Johnson, nicknamed Stella by Swift and by posterity, was a little girl of six years old when Swift first met her. She was a *protégée* of Sir William Temple's when Jonathan Swift acted as secretary and literary handy-man to that exalted gentleman long before his own ship had come home. The young parson's assorted duties included teaching Stella her letters. Probably he enjoyed it in that rather awesome household. He certainly did it efficiently, for she learnt to use a handwriting practically identical with his own, so that in later years friends who looked over Swift's post-bag used to joke him about writing to himself. She became his playmate and his friend, and she grew into something of the " little mother " for a man who, in spite of all his brilliance and his fame, was rather lonely and pathetically in need of mothering.

That is just the impression which one gets from Swift's " Journal to Stella "—a postal diary of the most artless prattling kind, in which he scribbled to her the kind of affectionate nonsense which one can only say to a real friend.

Exactly what Stella meant to Swift is set out charmingly in a happy little set of verses :

" When on my sickly couch I lay,
  Impatient both of night and day,
  Lamenting in unmanly strains,
  Call'd every power to ease my pains;
  Then Stella ran to my relief,
  With cheerful face and inward grief;
  And, though by Heaven's severe decree
  She suffers hourly more than me,
  No cruel master could require,
  From slaves employ'd for daily hire,
  What Stella, by her friendship warm'd,
  With vigour and delight perform'd."

Their friendship, be it said here and now, was an absolutely blameless one. One never sees Stella without her chaperon-shadow, Mrs. Dingley —nor did Swift, for that matter. Those two little ladies in rustling silk moved like twin sisters to soothe him when he was half crazy from beating his brains against abuses and corruption and cant. No one can point a finger of scandal at Stella— she was, rather, in the nature of Swift's good angel.

Now comes the crux, and the clue to the problem of Swift and Stella. The odd thing about Swift was his insurmountable fear of marriage. That was ingrained. It was something which he could not conquer, though he would. It was not a selfish fear so much as a psychological kink in Swift, combined with a shrinking dread of inherited madness. (His uncle, Godwin Swift, had died insane.) Jonathan Swift as much as confesses this trait himself.

> " With friendship and esteem possessed,
>   I ne'er admitted love a guest."

Yet for all that confirmed bachelordom, one thinks that Swift would willingly have given up his own life if only he could have spared Stella from some of the sufferings of her last illness in 1728. There is no doubt about his selfless affection for Stella, and we can not but believe him when he says to her that he

> " . . . gladly would your sufferings share,
>   Or give my scrap of life to you,
>   And think it far beneath your due;
>   You, to whose care so oft I owe
>   That I'm alive to tell you so."

And her death marked the end of Swift's happiness. It was the beginning of that horribly long and ghastly end which came to its most dreadful in stupor and squalor and insensibility. One hates to think of the poor old man holding on to life for another eighteen years, gradually getting deafer and more morose, and ending, if legend is true, in bestial oblivion as a shilling peepshow for the profit of his servants. How very much he loved her came out in the stricken starkness of that memoir of Stella which he wrote on the night that she lay in her coffin in the Cathedral, a stone's throw from his study.

Why they did at last marry, in 1716, is an obscure and lengthy story. Perhaps it is enough to say briefly here that Stella must have begun to feel her equivocal position keenly, and that in consequence the ceremony did take place, though never publicly announced.

They kept it a secret, and the wedding was the quietest one possible—but all the same it seems to have been an open secret. Swift's closest friend, Dr. Patrick Delaney, Fellow of Trinity College, and a member of the Dean's Cathedral chapter, never had any doubt about it. More than almost anyone else, Delaney was in a position to know. And Swift's Bishop, Dr. Evans of Meath, said quite plainly in a letter of July 27th, 1723, that Swift and Stella were man and wife.

There seems to be no real proof of the often suggested hint that a marriage was impossible and did not take place on account of a close relationship—that Swift and Stella were brother and sister, or, as Denis Johnson has suggested, uncle and niece. Denis Johnson's theory is admirably expressed, and every atom of relevant evidence is put forward with all the wily skill of a lawyer. But, in the opinion of this writer, his argument does not seem to prove his case conclusively, tempting and attractive and clever though it is. As to his belief about Swift's Temple parentage, it need not have been more than a coincidence that Sir John Temple happened to be a bencher of the King's Inns during the time previous to Swift's birth. Again, as for the commonly repeated piece of gossip, that Stella was Sir William's daughter, strong contrary evidence is supplied by a manuscript note by Orrery in a personal copy of his biography, dated September 14th, 1751.

> " Stella was the daughter of Sir William Temple's Steward. She was allowed by the Dean's sister (a bitter enemy of hers) to be the very picture of her mother's husband : and this Mrs. Fenton would insist on whenever she heard the aspersion of her being Sir William Temple's daughter mentioned, because, as she expressed herself, ' *she ought to give the devil his due* '."

For this significant piece of information we are indebted to an American student, Maxwell Gold, whose book, *Swift's Marriage to Stella* (Harvard, 1937), makes a strong case for the correctness of the marriage theory.

Undoubtedly there is a mass of testimony for the marriage, dating from Swift's own lifetime.

Delaney and Evans believed it, as we have said. So did Mrs. Sican, young Deane Swift, Mrs. Pilkington, and Orrery. Martha Whiteway stated that she was convinced that Stella was Swift's wife, and she was in a better position to be sure than most people. The earlier biographers followed the same lines—Dilworth, Hawkesworth, Dr. Johnson, Sheridan, Monck Berkeley, and Scott. The principal evidence on the other side is contained in Dr. Lyon's notes to Hawkesworth's life. But the balance of opinion of the eighteenth century was against him.

*   *   *

We may well accept, then, the truth of the traditional belief that they were married in 1716 by Dr. St. George Ashe, Bishop of Clogher, in the garden of his residence.

" Nonsense ! " says our sceptic, still sticking to his guns. " If there had been a wedding a record would have been kept of it. Where are Stella's marriage lines ? " The objection is not as convincing as it sounds. Eighteenth century weddings were apt to be hole and corner affairs. We all know how the Irish " couple-beggars " performed abduction ceremonies at the back of the bog, or to go to the other end of the scale, how secret weddings were performed at a moment's notice without any red tape in fashionable London churches.

One minister at the Savoy Chapel in London went as far as to issue an advertisement : " Marriages performed with the utmost Privacy, Secrecy, Decency and Regularity. There are five Private Ways by Land to this Chapel, and two by Water . . ." ! The garden wedding at Clogher reminds one of that ceremony performed by Swift under a tree in the Phoenix Park during a torrential deluge, and about which he made up a jingling rhyme :

" Under the oak in stormy weather
John George and Jane were wed together,
And only He who made the thunder
Can part John George and Jane asunder."

Such things did happen two hundred years ago when bureaucracy had not yet made people as register-minded as they are now !

*   *   *

" They were married and they lived happily ever after." That is the end of all good love stories. But it was a short " ever after " for poor Swift, who did not find over-much happiness in life. In 1728 Stella died, and Swift wrote a heart-broken little essay about her character that same evening and on the night of her funeral. It begins :

> "This day, being Sunday, January 28th, 1727, and about eight o'clock at night a servant brought me a note, with an account of the death of the truest, most virtuous, and valuable friend, that I or perhaps any other person ever was blessed with."

*   *   *

That, in brief, is the love story of Swift and Stella. And it is the firm conviction of the writer that but for Stella's influence, Swift could never have endured to be the great man and the great defender of his country that he was.

*   *   *

CADENUS AND VANESSA.

Now we come to the third member of the triangle—the vivid, passionate, baffled Vanessa. The curtain goes up this time in the London of Queen Anne to give us a glimpse of another schoolroom scene. It is in the red brick city home of Mrs. Vanhomrigh, that indefatigable hunter of social lions. She has taken up the interesting Dr. Swift, now a rising young ecclesiastical politician of forty-two, and in return for her hospitality he is educating her attractive seventeen-year-old daughter. They meet day by day and they drink coffee together in the little boudoir which they call " the sluttery " before turning to their books . . .

Now it so happened that Jonathan Swift quite enjoyed improving unformed minds. Also, he was unwary enough to believe that it was quite possible, without danger, to instruct a warm-blooded and beautiful girl young enough to be his daughter. That was where he was quite mistaken. It did not strike him that he could be a very attractive person himself. And so, while he looked on Vanessa as a friendly, docile little pupil whom he could teach and make a friend of, she for her part fell hopelessly and incurably in love with him.

For a while Swift failed to realise the truth, At first, even when he did, he did not take it very seriously. He liked Vanessa tremendously, but he loved Stella. And it was not until he discovered that Vanessa was fighting for love and marriage that he saw how unwisely he had acted.

Unfortunately, Swift, in the early stages of the affair, was not hard enough and cruel enough to make a complete breach. He came to Ireland to take up his post as Dean. The Irish Sea seemed to him a sufficient barrier against undue intimacy, and so he continued to answer her letters. Then Vanessa followed him and settled down at Celbridge—known in those days as

(41)

Kildrought. She was far too close to the Deanery for Swift's peace of mind—and Stella was looking on, too, from her cottage at Trim!

Needless to say, Swift was worried by the new move, and he did his best to induce Vanessa to return to London. But Vanessa kept fighting hard to win him and to hold him. Again and again she played on his compassion, knowing that he hated to give her pain. " Pray, what can be wrong in seeing and advising an unhappy young woman ? " she wrote. " You cannot but know that your frowns make my life insupportable."

In 1716 the rumour began to be whispered that Swift had married Stella. Poor baffled Vanessa's letters became more pleading and more tragic in their hopeless passion.

At last, in 1722, she decided to force Swift to choose between herself and Stella, writing to ask Stella whether she was married to the Dean or no. She was desperate, and it was a last gambler's throw. She was staking everything on this final attempt to force Swift's hand. And it failed utterly. For, white with anger, the Dean strode into her house at Celbridge and flung her letter back at her. It was the end. A few months later she died broken-hearted, having scored Swift's name out of her will.

*　　　*　　　*

It is a less sensational story than the tuppence-coloured picture of Swift's passionate relationships with Vanessa drawn by some writers. But we believe we have given the bare bones of what really did happen.

THE FORGOTTEN WOMAN

DEAR BRAINLESS DINGLEY !

THE Fat White Woman whom Nobody Loves is a pathetic and much-maligned person. Very few of us take the trouble to try to get to know her. She grows old and tired as the maiden aunt or companion-help who is tolerated but not regarded—a necessary nuisance who, in a fussy, brainless way, serves the more fortunate and gets very little thanks for it. The perfect example of the species is that dear, inarticulate, tea-cosy, Rebecca Dingley, life-long shadow-chaperon to Swift's Stella.

Nobody loves her. No writer except Alice Meynell has given her a page of biography all to herself. Every biographer of Swift has written excitedly and voluminously about the women who associated with the Dean. Stella ; the star-crossed Vanessa ; Varina, whom the young vicar of Laracor choked off so brutally with a letter to say that he would consider matrimony if her fortune were competent and her person cleanly; Letitia Pilkington, the shady little adventuress; Betty Jones of Leicester, whose hypothetical designs mother Swift foiled—they all appear in the printed page and everybody knows all about them. But who cares for poor Dingley ?

Nobody, apparently. Almost the only scrap of early biography available is an unchivalrous condemnation from Sheridan :

"The other lady, Mrs. Dingley, was far from meriting any share in Swift's esteem and affection. She was merely one of the common run of women, of a middling understanding without knowledge or taste; and so entirely selfish as to be incapable of any sincere friendship or warm attachment. In short, she was perfectly calculated to answer Swift's purpose in the post she occupied."

That ungentlemanly passage spoils Sheridan's *Life* for at least one reader, and by way of reaction it confirms Alice Meynell's plea that "No one else in literary history has been so defrauded of her honours. . . . The sentimentalist has fought against Mrs. Dingley from the outset. He has disliked her, shirked her, misconceived her and effaced her."

There is one fact which gives the lie to the

rather cruel verdict of posterity. Swift likes her.
Yes—the Gloomy Dean, who hates so many fools
and knaves, has a warm affection for poor Mistress Rebecca. It can be felt in one or two of
his poems. There is a gentle good humour in
his reference to her, which is reserved for few.
For example, there is that joint set of verses to
his dour old Presbyterian housekeeper, Mrs.
Brent, and to our comfortable, bustling, fussy,
busybody :

> Dingley and Brent
> Wherever they went
> Ne'er minded a word that was spoken;
> Whatever was said,
> They ne'er troubled their head,
> But laughed at their own silly joking.

Rebecca is one of those dear people eternally
busy doing little niggling bits of household work
which somehow never show much result. Here
she is, " healthy, fat and fair," sketched in a few
vivid strokes of Swift's economical pen :

> For though philosophers maintain
> The limbs are guided by the brain,
> Quite contrary Rebecca's led;
> Her hands and feet conduct her head;
> By arbitrary power convey her,
> She ne'er considers why or where :

Her hands may meddle, feet may wander,
Her head is but a mere by-stander :
And all her bustling but supplies
The part of wholesome exercise.

*　　　*　　　*

Mistress Dingley was apparently a cousin once removed of Sir William Temple's. She had been left with a tiny annuity of twenty-seven pounds a year, and in middle age became Stella's companion. In 1701, on Swift's advice, the two ladies moved to Ireland to live. In this country Stella could get ten per cent. on her £1,000 fortune; she would be near her County Wicklow farm, and provisions were cheap on this side of St. George's Channel. The vicarage of Laracor was always available for them when Swift was away from his parish, and in the intervals they could live in a cottage at Trim or as guests with Archdeacon Raymond. Dingley might not be a stimulating companion. Her favourite topics were weddings and funerals and christenings. When a burglar broke in, to be shot dead by Stella, Dingley would certainly put her head under the blankets and scream. But, in spite of Swift's jests, she was reliable and even useful in her muddled way. Any household accounts which survive are in her handwriting. She would see to the creature comforts of the *ménage*.

Only one example of her literary style survives, apart from her bookkeeping. This is a note to her brother, Bob, acknowledging the receipt of a bill for £108. It is just the kind of epistle we should expect of her, written in the hand of an unaccustomed scribe, who does as little correspondence as possible. Typically, it ends with the desperate excuse of one who can think of nothing else to say—" In hast from your Thankfull Sert. and affectionate Sister, Re. Dingley."

Perhaps in one thing she could outdo Stella—in spelling ! It is amusing to see that, in a receipt to Mr. Dingley, on the back of Rebecca's letter, Stella repeats her favourite and often-corrected error, " bussiness ! " Swift was never able to teach her to spell correctly. " Pray, Stella," he writes in the journal, " what do you mean by *Villian* and *Dainger*, and you, Madam Dingley, what is *Christianing?* " Apparently Rebecca is at her favourite topic again !

Wherever Swift went we find the quaint pair. Everybody knows that Swift never saw Stella without having Dingley present as well. In Quilca, that ramshackle farm where Sheridan lived, we meet the inseparables once more. Quilca was a happy-go-lucky house, with " Stools, Tables, Chairs and Bedsteds broke " ; a household where the servants

> Eat like a Turk,
>> Sleep like a Dormouse,
> Be last at work,
>> At Victuals foremost.

Dingley did not appreciate it at all. We can sympathise when we read some of the Dean's pen-pictures of the place :

> Grumbling, poor complaining Dingley
> Is left to care and trouble singly.

Its disorder fussed her chaotic brain, and she longed for the security of an ordered town house with shops round the corner. She "would rather live in a Dublin Cellar than in a Country Palace."

If we had not been told so specifically, we should still have known for certain that Mistress Dingley must have had a fat pet dog on which she doted. It was inevitable—and, of course, she had. It was called Tiger. Perhaps all her dogs for many generations kept the name of a first beloved pet. In 1741, Faulkner's *Dublin Journal* advertises an offer of "A Crown Reward and no Questions asked" to a finder who will return to "the Rev. Dr. Swift, Dean of St. Patrick's, or to the printer hereof," a "little Bitch of a Light Fox Colour with a round Head and long Ears," wearing a collar with the couplet :

Pray, steal me not, I'm Mrs. Dingley's
Whose Heart in this Four-footed Thing lies.

* * *

Mistress Dingley is, of course, immortalised
in the pages of the Journal. And, incidentally,
there is a trace of injustice in the popular title,
the " Journal to Stella." It was really a journal
to Stella and to Dingley. They are both in
Swift's mind. The nickname, " MD," does not
just stand for Stella alone. It means, perhaps,
" My Dears." At any rate, it is plural. If M
is Stella, then D is certainly Rebecca. Both are
in his mind when he writes. No honest reader
of the Journal can miss seeing his affection for
the shadowy member of the team—Dingley, for
whom he prays so often that she has her health
and no spleen, for whom he buys hinged spec-
tacles at Ludgate, and from whom he asks prayers
when he is suffering from his terrible giddy fits.

His care for her is rather touching. In later
life he even persuades her that she is entitled to
an annual payment from a mythical trust fund,
and demands formal receipts to camouflage the
fact that he is really paying her fifty guineas a
year out of his own pocket. By will he bequeaths
to her an annuity of twenty pounds from his
hospital funds. But Swift survived her, as he
survived all his generation. In 1743, two years

before his own death, Dingley had died, aged seventy-seven years.

Let us hope that his charming wish for the old age of the dear fussy old lady came true :

> And when she's in another scene,
> Stella long dead, but first the Dean,
> May fortune and her coffee get her
> Companions that will please her better :
> Whole afternoons will sit beside her,
> Nor for neglects or blunders chide her;
> A goodly set as can be found
> Of hearty gossips prating round;
> Fresh from a wedding or a christ'ning
> To teach her ears the art of list'ning,
> And please her more to hear them tattle
> Than the Dean storm, or Stella rattle.
>
> Late be her death, one gentle nod,
> When Hermes, waiting with his rod,
> Shall to Elysian fields invite her,
> Where there will be no cares to fright her.

THE THREE POETESSES OF DUBLIN

HAVE women figured more largely on the stage of Irish history than on that of other lands ? One suspects that they have, looking down the cavalcade of time. It is an imposing list. There is Grania of the Ships, that lusty western she-pirate who treated Queen Elizabeth's gift handkerchief with such bluff discourtesy. Or Lady Morgan, "The Wild Irish Girl," one of Dublin's celebrities, as Lever's lines bear witness :

> "Och, Dublin, sure, there is no doubtin',
>   Bates every city on the say;
> 'Tis there you find O'Connell spoutin'
>   And Lady Morgan makin' tay."

Or Speranza, Lady Wilde, the Poetess of The Nation, or Mrs. Delaney—the list is an unending one.

Nor is it just a political cavalcade. For women have stolen the Irish literary scene often enough, too. Maria Edgeworth's name jumps to the memory at once. Or, nearly a century earlier, that remarkable group of early 18th century Dublin women who earned fame as poets and scholars, and whom it is a pleasure here to recall from the past.

They were friends and *protégées* of Swift's, and the fiery Dean calls them his " poetical triumfeminate."

The most picturesque of them was the ingenious Letitia Pilkington, that lively and Bohemian poetess whose entertaining autobiography captures some of the most vivid pictures of Swift's Dublin days. These hastily-written volumes are full of glimpses of literary London; snapshots of high jinks in Swiftian Dublin and Georgian London and of low life in the Marshalsea debtor's prison; memories of Colley Cibber, kindest of men but most inefficient of poets laureate, " who wrote English only occasionally by mistake." She had a hard furrow to plough—that gay, penniless gossiping little poetess. She had an unspeakably bad husband and more than her share of worries. But she held her head high through it all, and somehow one cannot help respecting her courage in a hard world.

It is pleasant to know that in the last year or so before her death in 1750 (at the age of thirty-eight) she had quite a success in literary Dublin. For years she had scraped a precarious living as a literary hack, ghost writer, and composer of *billets doux* for love-lorn but illiterate bucks, with unashamed begging to fill in lean periods. Now, in 1748, a comedy of hers was acted successfully in the Little Theatre, Capel Street. People were beginning to like her poetry, some of which was charming. Guineas were pouring in apace for her tattling books of memoirs, which are now a storehouse of social history.

For Dubliners Mrs. Pilkington's chief interest lies in the fascinating informal pictures which she draws of Swift at home; of the Dean showing her an empty drawer to indicate just how much cash profit he had made from his poetry; of Swift suggesting to his cook that if she could not underdo an overdone roast, she should be more careful next time; of Swift tending his poor, giving away three hundred pounds a year in charity, and setting up a loan bank for poor tradesmen to buy tools and stock-in-trade.

*　　　　*　　　　*

Very like Mrs. Pilkington was Mrs. Barber whose poems caused a momentary flutter of interest among Dublin readers. Poor Letitia Pilkington was a little jealous of her—their trade were too alike for them to agree. Cattily enough she asserted that in spite of the revisions of Swift, Mrs. Grierson, Dr. Delaney and even herself, Mrs. Barber's poems were very soon to

be seen "in the Cheesemongers', Chandlers',
Pastry Cooks' and Second-hand Booksellers'
shops." And, indeed, all Swift's friendly influence and introductions to the great failed to keep
the wolf from her door. When she was down
and out she wrote to the Dean in great distress,
and one is happy to know that he presented her
with the highly saleable manuscripts of his
Polite Conversations—a useful gift to sell to a
publisher.

She was the first of that "Triumfeminate"
of Dublin business-men's wives whom the Dean
described in an interesting letter to Alexander
Pope, written in February, 1730 :

"There are three citizens' wives in this
town; one of them whose name is Grierson,
a Scottish bookseller's wife. She is a very
good Latin and Greek scholar and has lately
published a fine edition of *Tacitus*, with a
Latin dedication to the Lord Lieutenant ; and
she writes *carmina Anglicana non condemnanda.*
The second is one Mrs. Barber, wife to a
woollen draper, who is our chief poetess, and
upon the whole has no ill genius. I fancy I
have mentioned her to you formerly. The last
is the bearer hereof, and the wife of a surly
rich husband who checks her vein. . . . The
bearer's name is Sican. She has a very good
taste of poetry, has read much, and, as I hear,

has writ one or two things with applause which I never saw, except about six lines she sent me unknown with a piece of Sturgeon some years ago, on my birthday. . . . I give her this passport to have the honour and happiness of seeing you, because she has already seen the ostrich, which is the only rarity at present in this town, and her ambition is to boast of having been well received by you upon her return."

Mrs. Sican was the most prosperous and least poetical of the three. Or at least, if she did produce great poetry, the world has no more seen it than Swift did. Perhaps her surly husband suppressed her verses ! However, she was something better—a first-rate housekeeper with a palate for exotic foodstuffs. In addition to the birthday Royal Sturgeon we find her sending the Dean a present of Spanish Liquorice ! She is interesting, too, as a friend of Stella's, and one of the authorities who vouched for the fact of her marriage.

The last of the three " shopkeeper's wives " whom Swift considered " the only women of taste in Dublin," was Mrs. Grierson, who died aged twenty-seven, bowed down, we may suspect, under the burden of scholarship. She was the wife of the King's Printer in Ireland, whose books have a beauty of craftsmanship nowhere excelled in the eighteenth century. We have before us a Prayer Book printed by him at the Sign of the Two Bibles in Essex Street. It compares very favourably with the best Baskerville work.

George Grierson's young wife seems really to have deserved the extravagant praise she received, for her editions of *Terence* and *Tacitus* were genuinely good. Mrs. Pilkington has a lot to say about her. Now, critics tend to snap " Little Liar " at everything poor, dear Mrs. Pilkington ever wrote. But, in spite of her shady literary reputation, her *Memoirs* do contain a great deal of solid fact, and perhaps her judgment of Mrs. Grierson is not far from the truth after all. She remembers how Mrs. Grierson came as a flapper of eighteen to learn midwifery from her father, Dr. Van Lewen. " She was Mistress of Hebrew, Greek, Latin, and French, and understood the mathematics as well as most men : and what made these extraordinary talents yet more surprising was that her parents were poor illiterate country-people; so that her learning appeared like the gift poured out on the Apostles, of speaking all languages without the pains of study; or, like the intuitive knowledge of angels. . . She wrote elegantly, both in verse and prose; and some of the most delightful hours I ever passed were in the conversation of this female philosopher."

Swift was kind to his little triumfeminate—(a group curiously akin to those four men described as "The Three Musketeers!")—and they probably were all the more welcome to him because they had those bat-like treble voices which pierced his barrier of deafness.

Mrs. Pilkington, at least, has repaid her patron by giving some glimpses of Swift without which posterity would be the poorer. She had the gossip columnists' knack of catching the moment's impression and pinning it down for ever. Here, as a tail-piece, is one of her Deanery word-snapshots:

"Away the Dean walked, or rather, trotted, as hard as ever he could drive. I could not help laughing at his odd gait, for I thought to myself he had written so much in praise of horses that he was resolved to imitate them as nearly as he could. As I was indulging in this fancy, the Dean returned to me, and gave me a strong confirmation of his partiality to those animals: 'I have been considering, Madam, as I walked,' said he, 'what a fool Mr. Pilkington was to marry you, for he could have afforded to keep a horse for less money than you cost him. . . .

"The Dean shewed me into a little street-parlour (where sat his housekeeper, a matron-like gentlewoman, at work). ' Here,' says he : ' Mrs. Brent, take care of this child (meaning me) and see she does no mischief, while I take my walk out within doors.' The Deanery House has I know not how many pairs of back-stairs in it, the preceding Dean who built it, being, it seems, extremely fearful of fire, was resolved there should be many ways to escape in case of danger.

" The Dean then ran up the great-stairs, down one pair of back-stairs, up another, in so violent a manner that I could not help expressing my uneasiness to the good gentle-woman lest he should fall and be hurt. She said ' It was a customary exercise with him, when the weather would not permit him to walk abroad '."

A SUMMER'S JOURNEY IN 1723

Swift's Munster Tour.

EIGHTEENTH century anecdote reports that
when Dean Swift rode into Dublin from Laracor,
his feet firmly planted in great top-boots fastened
to the saddle, the slum dwellers who revered him
as the Drapier used to greet him with rousing
cheers and bring out bands to escort him to St.
Patrick's Close. In his lifetime he had become a
legend. He was a legend, not only in the slums
of the Coombe, but also all over Ireland. North,
south, east and west, the footprints of the wander-
ing Dean remain to this day. He penetrated to
the most remote highlands of the south, and in
the outlying fishing villages of the south, men
still remember the coming of the Drapier on
horseback.

By far the most obscure of all Swift's travels
was that undertaken in Munster during the
summer of 1723. It was obscure because he
refrained from leaving a track of correspondence
behind him. Apart from an extremely dull

Nature poem in Latin couplets he wrote practically nothing on this trip. And so the little that we know about this journey has to be conjectured and assembled painfully from tradition and from the reminiscences of his friends.

Perhaps the first reference to any trip in Munster is contained in a letter to Vanessa, dated May, 1719. In this the Dean says, writing in schoolboy French: "I shall go shortly to visit a gentleman, but I know yet neither the name nor the locality of his house." This person, the details about whose residence seem so vague in Swift's mind, was an eccentric ancestor of the Earls of Llandaff, who resided at Thomastown, the seat of the Mathew family. He was a man who prided himself on being the perfect host. His peculiar notion of hospitality made him efface himself entirely from his guests, who were encouraged to treat his house in every way as a hotel—except that they did not have to pay a bill. There was a free tavern, and a free coffee room and a free bowling green—in fact everything that a traveller could desire. Swift was so charmed with the place and with the comforts of its hospitality, and, one may even suspect, with its cheapness, that he stayed there for no less than four months.

Four years later Swift set out for a longer tour. Probably he felt it wise to be out of the range of the bitter tongues of Dublin gossip during that summer of 1723. He had broken finally with poor passionate baffled Vanessa. She did not forgive him, and in her final illness she had vented her pent-up resentment against Swift by cutting his name out of her will and by leaving all her property to an amiable stranger, Bishop Berkeley. All kinds of stories about Vanessa's relationship with Cadenus were swirling around the salons of Dublin. No matter if they were false; no matter if the unhappy Dean were the victim of nothing worse than his own vanity and lack of firmness. When she died rumour would rise to a frenzy of spite. Much better for Swift to keep out of the public eye for a while. To escape from the malicious chattering of polite conversation the Dean was timing his journey to begin in the middle of May. In a letter from Dublin, dated May 11th, 1723, he wrote to Robert Cope, saying: " I will tell you that for some years I have intended a southern journey, and this summer fixed for it, and I hope to set out in ten days. I never was in these parts "— that is, in the extreme south—" nor am acquainted with a Christian among them, so that I shall be little more than a passenger; from thence I go to the Bishop of Clonfert, who expects me and pretends to be prepared for me. . . . I may be in Clonfert by the middle of July." A little time passed before he actually set out. There were delays and set-backs. On the first of June he wrote again to Cope to say : " I go where I was never before, without one companion, and among people where I know no creature, and all this is to get a little exercise for curing a sore head." The reason sounds a little too ingenuous to be entirely true.

The next day Vanessa died. Swift decided to leave at once; to cut all his connections with Dublin and with his friends and to disappear without delay. No doubt he was wise. Writing long after midnight that same day to his friend, Knightley Chetwode, he added a hasty sentence to a business letter. " I am forced to leave town sooner than I expected." That was the last scrap of correspondence for fully two months.

Where did he go ? The first stage was Wood Park. Here we lose his tracks altogether. It may be that he stayed in Johnstown, Co. Kilkenny—there is a tradition at Johnstown Spa that he spent some nights at that pleasant little village. Thomastown would be another familiar port of call, though there is no certainty that he stayed there on his second tour. At any rate he was familiar with the aspect of Co. Tipperary. Nine years later he wrote a bitter description of the county to Dean Brandreth.

" I think I once was in your county, Tipperary,

which is like the rest of the whole kingdom, a bare face of nature, without houses or plantations; filthy cabins, miserable, tattered, half-starved creatures, scarce in human shape; one insolent oppressive squire to be found in twenty miles riding : a parish church to be found only in a summer's day journey, in comparison of which, an English farmer's barn is a cathedral; a bog of fifteen miles round; every meadow a slough, and every hill a mixture of rock, heath and marsh; and every male and female, from the farmer inclusive to the day labourer, infallibly a thief, and consequently a beggar, which in this island are terms convertible. The Shannon is rather a lake than a river, and has not the sixth part of the stream that runs under London Bridge. There is not an acre of land in Ireland turned to half its advantage yet it is better improved than the people; and all these evils are effects of the English tyranny, so your sons and grandsons will find out to their sorrow." What a typical sample of Swift's passionate indignation this is ! And may it not reflect the bitterness and agony of mind with which he rode southwards on that mournful trip, haunted always by the tragic ghost of a friendship gone sour; remembering always Vanessa dead and hating him—tortured Vanessa leaving her legacy of spite and disillusionment ?

Wherever he may have travelled, Swift seems to have missed any detailed exploration of Cashel. Years afterwards, when the black cloud of stupor was already beginning to overshadow his mind, his friend and former opponent, Archbishop Theophilus Bolton invited him to pay a first visit to see King Cormac's Chapel, " built beyond controversy above eight hundred years ago." The terms of Bolton's letter imply that Swift had never seen Cashel. Possibly it would seem it was by an alternative route that Swift eventually arrived at Cork City.

Here we are on firmer ground. We know that he was entertained to dinner by the Corporation. The curtain lifts for a moment to show a rival wit scoring off the Gloomy Dean. Swift was observed absent-mindedly pouring apple sauce over his duck. " Why," exclaimed the Cork humorist joyously, " the Dean eats his duck like a goose ! " The province had scored a point over the great Dubliner. The incident provides the atmosphere for Swift's sour description of the city. " Cork indeed was a place of trade, but for some years past is gone to decay, and the wretched merchants, instead of being dealers, are dwindled to pedlars and cheats." He did not love Cork. But on this unhappy pilgrimage, seeking forgetfulness, would he easily have loved any town or place ? Thirteen years later the

Mayor and Corporation, filled with patriotic zeal, and perhaps remembering his presence at their civic banquet, presented him with the freedom of the city, three members dissenting vigorously. The minutes of that body record that transaction briefly—" Revd. Deane Jonathan Swift in a silver box." He had not been generous with his praise of Cork, and Cork was economical towards him. The Reverend Dean was not particularly flattered. The Drapier might well have expected something better. Nine months later he wrote to Lord Orrery : " I am told by others as well as your Lordship that the City of Cork hath sent me my Silver Box and Freedom, but I know nothing of it . . . . when I get my Cork box I will certainly sell it for not being gold." In due course the casket did arrive, a full twelve-month after its granting, to be returned with more promptness than it had been sent because it bore no inscription. Ultimately the omission was remedied, and the last we hear of the casket is that it was left by will to a friend to keep his twist tobacco in. The wry wit of the Drapier had won the last round against the humorists of Cork.

Westward and still westward Swift rode during the long days of that summer of 1723. He passed by Protestant Bandon, pausing, so they say, to write a satirical tail to the notorious

diehard motto of that selectly populated town.
At last he reached the cliffs and fiords of Carbery
—beautiful, lonely, hospitable country. The soft
beauty of the best of Munster began to soothe
him. His host was a clergyman who had known
him, perhaps from a distance, when Swift had
first come to the Deanery ten years before. At
journey's end in the tower of Castlehaven, Swift
found a welcome from the Reverend Thomas
Somerville. There was a warmth in that tapes-
tried home before the logs blazing in that great
brass fireplace with its margin of blue Dutch
tiles. There was unfeigned friendship at last for
that tragic wanderer with the bark like an ill-
tempered dog. Thomas and his comfortable
wife, Anne, had the insight to see the burning
sincerity of one who was as honest as God's
angels underneath his pathetic sourness. The
shattered traveller began to thaw, began even to
find enjoyment in little boating excursions round
about the coast of Glandore and towards Balti-
more. He rambled and climbed among the
rocks and caves like a boy, so that on occasion
he had to be rescued from death on the jagged
cliffs by a couple of able-bodied servants. He
even tried to write Nature poetry. Dryden had
remarked years before : " Cousin Swift, you will
never be a poet." Dryden was quite right; the
corroded pen which could scratch the *Modest*

Proposal could not turn easily to the lyrical. Swift's *Rupes Carberiae* was definitely a very bad poem. But at least it shows that the old Swift who had loved the quicksets and the cherry-blossom of Laracor, was not quite dead. He was beginning to re-awaken a little to beauty. For a moment he was able to forget the jagged ugliness of life. Here is a fragment from Dr. Dunkin's prim little translation of some of Swift's poem, but no more stilted than the original thirty-four lines of prosaic Latin hexameters :

" Lo from the top of yonder cliff that shrouds
Its airy head amidst the azure clouds,
Hangs a huge fragment, destitute of props;
Prone on the waves the rocky ruin drops;
With hoarse rebuff the swelling seas rebound
From shore to shore the rocks return the sound."

The neighbouring families did their best to honour the traveller. They entertained him and asked him to dinner parties. But the mysterious gloom of the tragic visitor was hard to break down. Only once was it achieved. The occasion was at a dinner party given by Richard Townsend, when Swift really did laugh heartily for the first time since Vanessa's death. And the cause was the baiting of an unfortunate English sea captain, with an unhappily small sense of humour.

At last the time came to say farewell to Carbery, and to face his horse northwards. He was on his way to Clonfert. He was riding the hundred and twenty miles to the miniature cathedral city with its tiny church, the last blaze of the glory of Irish Romanesque. Where did he go ? The problem remains unsolved. But it does seem that he must have passed through the grey city of Limerick, under the shadow of King John's battered old fortress, and over the Shannon into the hills of Clare. For in the neat little village of Sixmile-bridge in that county, tradition has preserved a solitary footprint. It is one of those pointless legends so devoid of merit that only truth can justify them. Swift was staying, so they say, at the hostelry at Sixmilebridge. It was a Friday, and a notable day in that house in Catholic Clare, for there was a kind of church convention there, and the bishop and the dignitaries of the county were dining at the inn on fasting fare. Could Swift have meat for his dinner? The landlady was doubtful. She didn't quite like . . . . What would the Bishop think ? . . . . It didn't seem quite right to have the smell of cooking about the house just then . . . . Swift quite understood. But would she send a message from him to the Bishop ? Promptly he jotted down half a dozen lines of verse; lines adapted from the French; typical lines in their self-confident irony, Jove-like from habit, but good-humoured, and not intended to annoy :

> " Can any man of common sense
> Think eating meat gives God offence,
> Or that the herring hath a charm
> The Almighty's anger to disarm ?
> Wrapt up in majesty divine
> Does He reflect on what we dine ? "

The answer came at once. By all means the Dean of St. Patrick's was to have whatever he wished to eat. The elephantine playfulness of the Drapier met the courtesy of the Bishop. One likes to think that they saw one another and exchanged greetings.

Is this story true ? One can only say, like one of George A. Birmingham's characters, " It might be." *Prima facie*, there is no reason for not believing it. And if it really did happen, we can follow our lonely traveller northwards, through Ennis, past the blue hills of Slieve Aughty, along the Shannon by Portumna, and into the public eye again at the palace of Clonfert.

And so Swift came home. We need not dwell long on his stay at Clonfert. At any rate he saw enough of it and of its surrounding diocese to write scurrilously about it to his crony Sheridan —that humorous, luckless, schoolmaster-divine— and to advise him not to seek preferment there, wherever else he might try. In this letter, dated the third of August, and concerning his return, Swift says : " No, I cannot possibly be with you so soon; there are too many rivers, bogs and mountains between; besides, when I leave this, I shall make one or two short visits in my way to Dublin, and hope to be in town by the end of this month. . . . If you are for a curacy of twenty-five pounds a year, and ride five miles every Sunday to preach to six beggars, have at you; and yet this is no ill country, and the bishop has made, in four months, twelve miles of ditches from his house to the Shannon, if you talk of improving."

The circle completes itself. By the twentieth of September he is back in Dublin, and he is writing to Alexander Pope to tell him that he has travelled over four hundred miles on " a summer expedition of four months on account of my health." Some day perhaps we may find a series of letters to tell us more about what happened during those summer weeks. Till then, the Munster visit remains one of the most baffling and obscure episodes in the career of Swift.

GULLIVER WAS A CAVAN MAN

IN the year 1711, Jonathan Swift was writing down the outlines of an imaginary world tour by a certain Martinus Scriblerus.

Fascinating they promised to be, these travels which took place in 1699, and very tantalising in their presentation :

"Thou shalt know then, that in his first Voyage he was carry'd by a prosperous Storm to a Discovery of the Remains of the ancient Pygmæan Empire.

"That in his second, he was as happily shipwreck'd on the land of the Giants, now the most humane people in the world.

"That in his third Voyage, he discover'd a whole Kingdom of Philosophers, who govern by the Mathematicks; with whose admirable Schemes and Projects he return'd to benefit his own dear country. . . ."

The story of Martinus did not reach the public eye until 1726, and in the interval the hero had changed his name to Lemuel Gulliver, ship's surgeon, who resided with his wife and family near the docks of Wapping.

In the Dublin of 1726, hasty editions of *Gulliver* were being devoured by the public. That delightfully circumstantial yarn, which has added words to our vocabulary like "Yahoo" and "Lilliputian," was on everyone's lips. Readers were even persuaded of the actual truth of the story. There were people who strained their eyesight trying to discover the island of Lilliput on the map.

A certain sea captain claimed to be an intimate friend of Dr. Lemuel Gulliver, but said that his residence was at Rotherhithe, and not at Wapping. An Irish Bishop was sufficiently convinced of the general authenticity of the story to complain about the lies which it contained!

And for 219 years the *Travels of Captain Lemuel Gulliver into Several Remote Nations of the World* have continued to be "a tale which holdeth children from their play and old men from the chimney-corner."

The curious thing is that there was a real Gulliver, and that he was an Irishman. But he was a farmer, and not a sailor, and Jonathan Swift made his acquaintance, not on the Liffey docks, but on the plains of County Cavan. His name was "Big" Doughty.

It was Swift's custom for several years to pass

his summer holidays in the parish of Mullagh in the County of Cavan, near Virginia Water. It was by way of a picnic holiday, this stay with his companion wit, Dr. Thomas Sheridan, at Quilca House. For the Quilca farm was a kind of minor Castle Rackrent; the windows were broken; the beds were shaky; the doors had no handles, and the roof was ready to fall in at any moment.

Sheridan had a shrewish wife, but to compensate for that he had a sense of humour and the amiable procrastinations of a Mr. Micawber, that on to-morrow or the day after something might turn up. In other words, he was an ideal holiday companion, and Dean Swift loved to potter about his wilderness of a garden and exchange puns for a few weeks in the summer without having to think of affairs of state.

Nearby there lived a farmer with the physique of a Hercules. He was a kind of local legend, and a famous " playboy "—" Big " Doughty he was called, a member of a very respectable family which still survives in the neighbourhood.

For the benefit of travellers, " Big " Doughty loved to show off his prowess. He was of tremendous strength and of colossal size. On one occasion he rescued from a process-server a fellow-farmer (who, like most farmers, was in financial difficulties) by the expedient of hiding him under the skirts of his overcoat until the danger had passed.

With equal good nature he lifted a poor widow's cow out of the village pound, where it had been imprisoned for straying, and delivered it safely back to its mistress. And for the great Dean from Dublin he gave an exhibition of what he could do, on one summer afternoon. The high-light of this show of strength was to carry a young horse from one field to another across a fence—an exploit which impressed the holiday-making Dean tremendously !

Here is where Gulliver comes in. A good many years previously, as we have seen, Swift had been playing with the idea of writing an imaginary tour in which his hero was to discover the remains of the " ancient Pygmæan Empire." When he saw " Big " Doughty (so the local tradition still says), the idea came back to him. The result was the completion of *Gulliver's Travels*, part of which was actually penned on a rath on the Quilca estate.

"POOR PROJECTING POCKRICH"

A Swift Contemporary who might have belonged to the Grand Academy of Lagado

LEWIS CARROLL says in one of his nonsense rhymes :

> I was thinking of a plan
> To dye one's whiskers green
> And always use so large a fan
> That they could not be seen.
>
> But I was thinking of a way
> To feed oneself on batter
> And so go on from day to day
> Getting a little fatter.

One may use these verses from *Alice Through the Looking Glass* as a kind of motto or theme song for Richard Pockrich, the Dublin inventor who died in 1759.

During the 18th century most of our eccentrics seem to have concentrated on being inventors. In those days Dublin was certainly the home of surprisingly many crack-brained projectors, as they were called. They were benevolent, well-meaning people. They had great vision, if not so great achievement. The worst you can say of them is that most unkind of remarks : " They meant well." I can't altogether forgive Swift for satirising them so cruelly in Gulliver's visit to the Grand Academy of Lagado. Do you remember the list of crazy inventions he gives in that passage—the man who planned to extract concentrated sunshine from cucumbers; the ingenious architect who contrived to build houses from the roof downwards rather than from the foundation upwards; the breeder of naked sheep; the textile experimenter who was inducing spiders to produce coloured cobwebs, and so forth ?

I suspect our hero, poor Richard Pockrich, was the origin of most of Swift's buffoonery, just as he was the ancestor of all projectors like Lewis Carroll's White Knight, who remarked : " The more head downwards I am the more I invent new things."

Actually, our fat jovial little man in the bag wig was not nearly such a figure of fun as his contemporaries thought. Many of his ideas were very sound, but they were 200 years ahead of his time—blood transfusion, flying machines, iron boats and so on.

His fame rests principally on queer musical

instruments. First came his one-man-band of twenty drums of different pitch, which he ranged round himself in a circle and played in xylophone fashion. Then there was his pin-and-wire instrument—a kind of rough and ready dulcimer. This gadget must have made Pockrich a decidedly worrying guest, particularly if the furniture was valuable. For on the slightest hint he seems to have been ready to whip a hammer and nails and a roll of wire from his pocket, and would set to work driving the nails into the nearest table. In a few minutes the instrument was rigged up, ready to play music of his own composition.

But by far the most famous and successful of his instruments were the musical glasses, or, as he called them without any false modesty, " the Angelic Organ." This invention consisted of a set of glass goblets, of different sizes and depths, filled with varying quantities of water to tune them to the correct pitch. Very pleasant musical effects were obtained on these. Pockrich used to play elaborate pieces by Handel, and they became a popular craze at the period. As the Vicar of Wakefield remarks, the pet topics of fashionable conversation in the middle of the 18th century included Shakespeare, pictures, and the musical glasses, which certainly puts them in high company !

They were, in fact, poor Pockrich's most

profitable and successful invention. It seems a pity that he never did actually face the examiners of Trinity College with this new instrument. His ambition was to sit for his Doctorate of Music, presenting to the University a selection of his own compositions played by himself on his own invention. He might well have been successful. He was an excellent musician, and his little instrument had a charming tone which attracted composers like Beethoven, Mozart, and I should like to have seen him achieve his ambition.

I am afraid that sometimes our poor projector was not as sober as he should have been. Whether this was the cause or the effect of his having started a brewery at Islandbridge I do not know. What is certain is, that it was not successful. He failed to win the R.D.S. prize for the best barrel of porter—which was a Dublin speciality even in those days—and eventually the whole concern lost him a good deal of his capital. Still less profitable was his plan for covering Ireland with vineyards. His scheme for draining and tilling the bogs was a far more sound project —but, alas, the public only laughed at it. The pathetic thing is that there was a great deal of sound theory in many of his ideas—it was in practical detail that they seemed to go wrong.

Such, for instance, was his goose-raising industry. He spent a good deal of money in buying some thousands of acres of moor and mountain in County Wicklow, planning to breed geese in such quantities that he could capture the English and the European markets. But again something went wrong. Sufficient capital was not forthcoming, the geese did not flourish as they should have, and the markets did not open up as expected. Poor Pockrich !

As we may expect, his medical prescriptions were many, varied and odd. But one scheme is of startling interest to-day—his idea of the value of blood transfusion. He was firmly convinced that if he could cause young and healthy blood to flow into the veins of the feeble, wonderful things would happen. In this he was quite right, of course. But he went too far in asserting that blood transfusion would guarantee immortality. Even 18th century Dublin could not believe that ! But a few insurance companies and heirs waiting on the death of rich relations were quite seriously perturbed. Pockrich did his best to pacify these folk by promising to secure an Act of Parliament enabling the beneficiaries to claim their rights when the rejuvenated patients had reached a certain statutory age !

Then there was his project to erect an observatory on the top of one of the Wicklow mountains. And his really excellent idea for providing men-of-war with unsinkable iron lifeboats, or even of having all-iron ships. In the face of the jesting of all his contemporaries, he never ceased to look forward to a time when the seafaring nations would abandon oak in favour of iron.

We keep getting glimpses of Pockrich all over Dublin.

We pick up a faint trail at Old St. Audoen's Church, in Dame Street, whose tower in the 18th century housed successively the Guild of Tanners and, in 1764, the first printing office of a very venerable Irish newspaper. (I regret to say that a rival proprietor, George Faulkner, Swift's printer, called it—

That disgrace to law and reason,
That mass of slander, dullness, treason,
That journal which the arch produces.

So I cannot very well name the journal here !)
However, that is by the way. Thus St. Audoen's Parish Records tell how—

" The famous Flying Man flew twice, in a very extraordinary manner, from the top of King John's Castle in Thomas Street, to a post set up in Meath Street."

Who was the flying man ? Nobody knows now. But we do know this much—that Pockrich was living in Dublin at the time, and that his mind was very much occupied with the thought of flying. He believed that one day, as he said, men would call for their wings in the same casual voice with which in the seventeen hundreds they called for a pair of boots ! So it may well be that Pockrich did actually succeed in a gliding experiment, bringing to Dublin the credit for perhaps the first successful flight ever.

Poor projecting Pockrich deserved at least the satisfaction of being laid to rest in the highly ingenious manner which he had wished. It was to have been a last experiment in embalming. He had devised a massive airtight leaden coffin for himself, which was to be filled with spirits of his own concoction, made to his own secret formula. Alas—this was his final failure. For on a certain Saturday in 1759, death came suddenly—he was burned to death in London !

THOMAS PARNELL, THE POET

A Friend of the Scriblerus Club

FROM the pages of a Dublin printed volume of 1773 the face of a young divine in wig and bands is looking out amiably and rather inquisitively from a little line engraving. It is a particularly attractive face, without one atom of pride or stiffness. Frank wide-set eyes; humorous lips with a pleasant lift at the corners. The face of Dr. Johnson's "clubbable" man—a friendly and fundamentally good person.

It is Thomas Parnell—one of our lesser Anglo-Irish poets by our twentieth century way of thinking, but a writer whose charm and achievements linked him closely with the great minds of the early eighteenth century, and who achieved a gigantic reputation for his tiny output. He was a poet whose verse had something of the fresh and healthy-minded youthful normality which suffuses Rupert Brooke's works, and which is so largely the secret of Brooke's popularity. Like Brooke, too, he died young before the fresh sparkle of his genius had been tarnished. For he did not live long enough to spoil his reputation. The dark demon of melancholia and mental instability which dogged the Parnell family, and which haunted Charles Stewart as well as Thomas, failed to touch his verse.

If the tag " show me your friends and I'll tell you the kind of man you are " has any validity at all, Parnell should rank high as a personality. He was intimate with both Steele and Addison, and managed to retain their friendship though he was an associate of the stalwarts of the opposite political party—no easy achievement in days of full-blooded political hatreds ! He assisted the *Guardian* and the *Spectator* with allegorical papers which at least filled a gap pleasantly, though they are no longer very readable. He was the companion of Swift and Alexander Pope, entrusted with the writing of the prefatory essay to Pope's *Iliad*, and honoured with a complimentary set of verses. He was a member of that famous literary coterie, the Scriblerus Club, which had been started to ridicule pedantry and " all the false tastes in learning." This amiable and not-too-serious brotherhood brought him into collaboration with Arbuthnot, the wit and main-spring of the group; Pope; Gay, the rising poet and future author of the *Beggars' Opera;* and the ironical Dean himself; with

Jervas, the Irish portrait painter, and Oxford coming in as honorary non-practising members. (Of the group, Oxford wrote gracefully :

> " He that cares not to rule will be sure to
> obey,
> When summoned by Arbuthnot, Pope,
> Parnell and Gay.")

He was accounted in his day one of the masters of English poetry. His biography was included in Johnson's *Lives of the Poets*. Goldsmith compiled another Life. Johnson wrote his epitaph. So did Goldsmith, very pleasantly.

> " This tomb, inscribed to gentle Parnell's name
> May speak our gratitude, but not his fame.
> What heart but feels his sweetly moral lay
> That leads to truth through pleasure's
> flowery way
> Celestial themes confess his tuneful aid;
> And Heaven, that lent him genius, was
> repaid.
> Needless to him the tribute we bestow,
> The transitory breath of fame below :
> More lasting rapture from his works shall rise,
> While converts thank their poet in the skies."

Before we try to estimate the value of his verse writings we had better chronicle the few relevant details of his life. In 1679 Thomas Parnell,

brother of Lord Justice John Parnell, who was
Charles Stewart Parnell's ancestor, was born in
Dublin. He seems to have been a scholarly
child, even discounting the prodigy stories which
are invented about all eminent men from the
fond memory of their old nurses. For he
entered Trinity College, Dublin, at the age of
thirteen—juvenile even in a century when the
age of the average university student was lower
than it is now. He certainly had gained a reputation as a promising classicist by the time he
graduated at the age of twenty-one. When he
was twenty-five he was appointed Archdeacon
of Clogher by Bishop St. George Ashe. And in
1716, two years before an early death, he became
Vicar of Finglas.

Such are the bare bones of the career of the
poet—dull and quiet enough. He was a man
who appeared on the literary stage in mere
glimpses. A shy man, and the victim of periods
of melancholy, when he retired to recuperate in
the Irish countryside, the spotlight of history
focuses on his association with the Scriblerus
group. He was one of Swift's *protégés*—like
many an other worse poet. (The Dean attracted
all kinds of writers, like the poet, Diaper, "the
poor little short wretch," whom he found starving
in a garret and helped, or that Mrs. Barber,
whom Swift publicised generously and rather

undiscriminatingly, and to whom he presented the profits of the *Polite Conversations;* or Mrs. Pilkington, the pathetic little scandal-mongering adventuress; or the broken-down Captain Creighton, for whom Swift compiled a highly-saleable book of memoirs). Parnell was in a different category. He had moderate wealth, and good position; he carried an introduction from Dilly Ashe, and Swift's " little friendly forwarding " gave him an entry into literary London. On Christmas Day, 1712, he brought Parnell to dine with Bolingbroke and wrote enthusiastically about him to Stella that night : " I carried Parnell to dine at Lord Bolingbroke, and he behaved himself very well, and Bolingbroke is mighty pleased with him." A year previously Swift had written sympathetically : " I am heartily sorry for poor Mrs. Parnell's death; she seemed to be an excellent and good-natured young woman, and I believe the poor lad is much afflicted; they appeared to live perfectly well together." It was true. Parnell never recovered from the loss of his wife. Nearly a year afterwards Swift wrote feelingly : " He has been ill with grief of his wife's death," and his bereavement hastened his end. Swift's pity increased his generous appreciation of Parnell's work. ' He passes all the poets of the day by a bar's length," he wrote—strong words when we re-

member the galaxy of genius which ornamented
the literary firmament of Queen Anne's day.

In his friendship Swift was loyal. The
moment he had been appointed to the Deanery of
St. Patrick's in 1713 he wrote to Archbishop
King to beg the reversion of his prebend of
Dunlavin for Parnell. King's reply was cautious.
Obviously he meant to keep as firm a hand as
possible on the stormy petrel who was coming
to St. Patrick's. So the Archbishop excused
himself coldly enough, and ended by changing
the subject and recommending Swift to go ahead
with the project for building a brick spire on the
tower of St. Patrick's. " Irish brick will do very
well." Happily Swift was independent enough
to stave off the monstrosity for the forty-five
years of his tenure !

Goldsmith preserves one quaint anecdote in
which Swift and Parnell both feature. It appears
that the Scriblerus Club was in the habit of
tramping into the country around London.
Swift was always the butt of all practical jokes.
The whole group agreed to walk down to the
country seat of a certain nobleman, twelve miles
from the city. The excursion took the form of
a walking race, with Swift—a tireless walker—
leading easily and quite determined to pick the
most comfortable bed when he arrived. However, Parnell decided otherwise, and arrived of

horseback by another way long before him. And
so a plan was concocted to keep Swift out of
both the best bed and also the house. Swift had
never had smallpox, and was very nervous of
catching it. So, as soon as his long legs were
seen striding up to the house, a footman was
sent out to say that the house was in quarantine
and that the family were all laid up; however,
a summer-house at the end of the garden, pro-
vided with a camp bed, was at his service. There
the poor Dean was obliged to retire and take a
cold supper which was sent out to him, while
the rest of the party were feasting within. However, at last they took compassion on him, and
when they secured his promise never to choose
the best bed again they allowed him to join them.

It is sad that melancholy at last took its toll of
the amiable poet. The joyousness vanished
which could write the Spring-like stanzas of his
Hesiod :

> " My days have been so wondrous free
>   The little birds that fly
> With careless ease from tree to tree
>   Were but as blest as I.
>
> Ask gliding waters if a tear
>   Of mine increased their stream ?
> Or ask the flying gales if e'er
>   I lent one sigh to them ? "

The death of his wife was almost the end
Sorrow—morbid grief—and the drowning of it—
did their work. In July, 1718, he died suddenl
in Chester on his way back to Ireland. Hi
body lies in Trinity Church in the old city
where an unobtrusive memorial is to be foun
by the diligent searcher.

*　　　*　　　*

What can be said of his verse ? Much of i
is pleasant, but to our modern ears little of i
rises beyond an amiable and slick classical neat
ness—the result of hard work by Parnell and
much suggestion by his more gifted friends
One of the happy exceptions is his *Anacreontic*
where his picture of the drunken feast of th
gods has all the junketing *bonhomie* of Horac
and the delightful formal rusticity of a Wattea
painting. The verse which tells of the dis
gruntled retirement of bibulous Comus from
teasing Olympus is a little gem :

> " And Comus, loudly cursing wit,
> 　　Roll'd off to some retreat
> Where boon companions gravely sit
> 　　In fat unwieldly state."

" Fat Unwieldly State ! " With what economy
he sketches a perfect word picture !
Then there was his *Fairy Tale*, in " Th

Antient English Style," so popular in a day when imitation Gothic ruins were coming to be all the rage. Alas!—to a generation which understands Gothic, it is as patently sham as the most castellated and barbicanned Scottish Pseudo-Baronial keep ever plastered over a decent Regency residence.

His *Hermit* is better. At least there is an ingenious and high moral story in it, borrowed from the Koran *via* Spain. To do it justice, it is an extremely effective allegory on the problem of suffering. It certainly was eagerly devoured by the public, going through edition after edition, and inspiring Bewick to illustrate it with some of his finest woodcuts. The subject fitted in perfectly with current literary fashion. Hermits were popular garden ornaments in the eighteenth century. Salaried anchorites lurked in caves in the grounds of baronets, holding hour-glasses in their hands, wearing long beards, and faithfully refusing to accept half-crowns from visitors. As a profession the job of being a hermit was seriously considered—witness the advertisement columns of the eighteenth century press. No really first-rate eighteenth century Capability Brown Garden was complete without a romantically neglected ancient living on nuts and berries. So any poem which began as Parnell's did was bound to please :

" Far in a wild, unknown to public view,
  From youth to age a rev'rend hermit grew;
  The moss his bed, the cave his humble cell,
  His food the fruits, his drink the chrystal
      well :
  Remote from man, with God he pass'd the
      days,
  Pray'r all his business, all his pleasure praise."

This is attractive, but no one could call it
important. But Parnell does step across the
division which separates synthetic Gothic or
Augustan slickness from genuine inspiration when
he writes his *Night Piece on Death*. It is a great
poem, and we use the word " great " with a full
consciousness of what it means. There is a
section in it which rivals the magic of

" Sceptre and crown must tumble down
  And in the dust be equal made
  With the poor crooked scythe and spade."

That is the passage where the hollow voice of
Death is heard speaking from among the bones :

" When men my scythe and darts supply,
  How great a King of Fears am I !
  They view me like the last of things;
  They make, and then they dread my stings.
  Fools ! If you less provoked your fears,
  No more my spectre-form appears.

Death's but a path that must be trod,
If man would ever pass to God :
A port of calms, a state of ease
From the rough rage of swelling seas."

Centuries previously the Chinese sage Chuang Tzu expressed that thought when he said : " How do I know that hating to die is not like thinking one has lost one's way, when all the time one is on the path that leads home ? "

There is power and passion in the lines which follow, picturing the trappings of the eighteenth century funeral. Parnell here is no longer the amiable Horatian. He has achieved something of the prophet's fire, something of the personal emotion which, for example, makes Van Gogh's paintings vital.

" Why then thy flowing sable stoles,
    Deep pendent cypress, mourning poles,
    Loose scarfs to fall athwart thy weeds,
    Long palls, drawn herses, covered steeds,
    And plumes of black, that as they tread,
    Nod o'er the escutcheons of the dead ? "

Just so did William Allingham feel when he wrote some of his best lines :

" No funeral gloom, my dears, when I am gone ;
    Corpse gazings, tears, black raiment, grave-
        yard grimness ;
    Think of me as withdrawn into the dimness,

> Yours still, you mine. Remember all the best
> Of our past moments, and forget the rest,
> And so to where I wait, come gently on."

A vivid and luminous confidence lights up the closing passage of Parnell's greatest poem :—

> " Nor can the parted body know,
> Nor wants the soul, these forms of woe :
> As men who long in prison dwell,
> With lamps that glimmer round the cell,
> Whene'er their suffering years are run,
> Spring forth to greet the glittering sun;
> Such joy, though far transcending sense,
> Have pious souls at parting hence.
> On earth, and in the body placed,
> A few and evil years they waste;
> But when their chains are cast aside,
> See the glad scene unfolding wide,
> Clap the glad wing, and tower away,
> And mingle with the blaze of day."

After a rather artificial and pseudo-gothic beginning of livid light and charnel-houses, this *Night Piece* rises in these closing thirty lines to a level which places it high among the great poems of life and death and immortality. If only for this poem, Parnell's reputation is secure.

"LOVE IS NOTHING ELSE BUT PRIDE"

A Stray Poem from Swift's Pen?

*Three years ago Mr. Seumas O'Sullivan showed
the writer an interesting and tantalising poem
which he had found. It purports to have been
written by Swift, and since it has been out of
print for nearly two centuries it may be worth
publishing again "to oblige the Public."*

THIS poem is printed in a Dublin newspaper
issued in the year 1773, as a fragment of advertisement on the reverse side of the leaf shows.
The publication seems to be *Faulkner's Penny
Journal*, and, since Faulkner succeeded Harding
as Swift's publisher, it is quite likely that this
poem may have long remained unnoticed or
forgotten in the printer's office. The contributor
boldly attributes the authorship to "the late
Dean Swift," and asserts that it has not previously
been published. At any rate, it does not appear
in any of the collections of Swift's works, and

careful search has failed to trace its existence elsewhere. Here is a reprint of the whole page exactly as it stands :

" The following Poem of the late Dean Swift has never yet been published. By inserting it in your useful and amusing Paper you will oblige the Public, and   *A constant Friend.*

> *La Cause pourquoi Deux Amants ne s'ennyient point, c'est parce qu'ills parlent toujours d'eux mesmes.*
>   *Maximes de Mons. de la Rochfacauld.*

A Maxim of Rochfacault's *by Dean* Swift.

> Wise Rochfacault has scarce assigned
> One Virtue to the human Mind.
> I mean a Virtue pure, unmixt,
> Without a Growth of Vice betwixt.
> Our Actions, Passions, thro' his Quill
> Are fairly annalysed to Ill.
> His Maxims say, (where'er he got 'em)
> That Vice is lurking at the Bottom.
>
> His o'ergrown Satire does not spare
> The Brave, the Gen'rous, or the Fair.
> Yet most I marvel what cou'd move,
> His witty Malice against Love;
> For hear him wickedly decide,
> That Love is nothing else but Pride.

" The Cause why Lovers when alone,
" Are never tir'd is easily shewn;
" For trace it to it's genuine Source,
" Self is the Subject of Discourse."

I'll not uphold the Maxim true,
I but illustrate what he drew.

The harmless Virgin just begun
Through female Fopperies to run,
Frequents the Opera, Park and Play,
Sees the same Faces ev'ry Day;
Her Heart ne'er entertains a Spark;
She loves the Opera, Play and Park.
But let a Youth with Wealth endowed,
Distinguish her amidst the Crowd,
Commend her Shape, Complexion, Eyes,
And teach her how herself to prize,
Strange Thoughts within her Bosom move,
And Pride will kindle into Love.

Damon a Youth for Celia sighs,
His Fortune of a middle Size,
His Character exempt from Blame
Clear as the Stock from whence he came,
Nor Envy's self his Virtue wounds;
But Celia has six Thousand Pounds.
From whence 'tis plain her Right is clear,
To have six Hundred Pounds a Year;

And Marriage Settlements provide,
For ev'ry Chance that may betide.
No Girl will yield, tho' e'er so raw,
The Usury allow'd by Law.—
Damon in vain may speak his Pains;
PRIDE enters, and forbids the Bans.

The friendly Law makes all Things common
Betwixt the Man and his good Woman,
As tho' in Wedlock were design'd
A secret Unison of Mind,
That if the Partner's Heart shou'd ache,
The corresponding Heart must shake,
As coupl'd by some magic Tie :—
Experience gives the Law the Lye :
For grant them plighted Heart for Heart,
And Hymen has perform'd his Part,
Connubial Love ne'er claims her Thought—
But what she costs, and what she brought;
Her Head a Chaos wild becomes,
Of Dress, and Equipage, and Drums,
And Servants silver-liv'ried o'er,
And fifty Thousand Follies more.

In rural Scenes, remote from Art,
Where Nature better plays her Part,
The frisking Baggage full of Glee,
That scarce has conn'd her A.B.C.
Throws out her Nets around the Plain,
To catch the Heart of amorous Swain;

Nor can she give her Conquests o'er,
Till stock'd with Lovers Half a Score;
Nor knows she then on which to fix,
But plays on all her jilting Tricks.
Meantime, beneath the Hedge-row Green,
He scarce a Youth, and *she* Sixteen,
A little Elf, with beardless Chin,
Teaches, and learns of her to Sin,
Secure they crop the barren Joy,
And taste the Bliss without Alloy.

Wise *Rochfacault*, you well decide,
That Love is nothing else but Pride.

It is the business of the critic to try to analyse
such a poem in order to test its authenticity.
Can it really be assigned to the Dean ? The
quality is not very high, but nevertheless can it
be a genuine relic from those sheaves of Swift
manuscripts which found their way into print in
the highways and byways of eighteenth century
publishing ? We know that his output in later
years was immense, and on occasions rather
mechanical. In his " Lines on the Death of Dr.
Swift " he refers to these stacks of material :

" Now Curll his shop from rubbish drains;
Three genuine tomes of Swift remains ! "

Stray poems and epigrams and squibs of all
kinds found their way into the hands of enter-

prising printers and hosts of acquaintances like Sheridan and Mrs. Barber and Mrs. Pilkington. The Dean's love of mystery kept him from admitting the authenticity of many pieces attributed to him. He has asserted that he has borne the reproach of many hundreds of printed papers that he had never seen. Undoubtedly he had his ardent imitators. But on the whole, if we accept the opinion of Elrington Ball, the vast majority of pieces attributed to him did owe their origin at least to his inspiration, if not actually to his pen. So far, then, there is not the slightest reason for doubting the authenticity of this piece. Indeed, the testimony of its publisher makes out a *prima facie* case in its favour.

Can it be assigned to any definite period of Swift's life ? Whether it is genuine or derivative, there is a probability that it may be assigned to the period after Stella's death, or sometime about 1730 at earliest. Closer dating is difficult, as there are no personal allusions of any kind. In itself this is a suspicious factor as regards authenticity, for despite his protests that

> " . . . . malice never was his aim,
> He lash'd the vice but spared the name,"

he rarely refrained from introducing personalities A Swift poem without topical allusions is rare indeed. One clue, however, there is. The quotation from Rochefoucauld and the manner of its introduction recalls strongly the introduction of Faulkner's Dublin edition of the lines on his death.

> " Verses on the Death of Dr. S——, D.S.P.D. Occasioned By reading a Maxim of Rochefoucault. *Dans l'adversitié de nos meilleurs amis nous trouvons quelque chose, qui ne nous deplaist pas.* In the Adversity of our best Friends, we find something that doth not displease us. Written by Himself, November 1731.
> London Printed : Dublin : Re-printed by George Faulkner. M,DCC,XXXIX."

There is no doubt that the author of our poem knows these lines. But whether this suggests authenticity, or merely studied imitation after the manner of one of the Dean's best known poems must be a matter of opinion.

The thought and philosophy of the whole set of verses follows the trend of Swift's later ideas very closely. Here, for example we find the notorious revulsion against chivalry which distorted his outlook on love and marriage. Though nowhere as ugly or unprintable as in some of his later pathological verses, the attitude of unwillingly fascinated disgust is there quite clearly. We see the mind of an author who hates marriage,

yet cannot keep his thoughts away from it. The
1728 edition of *Thoughts on Various Subjects*
contains the aphorism " What they do in Heaven
we are ignorant of; what they do not we are
told expressly, That they neither marry nor are
given in marriage." The celibacy which could
write in 1721 :

> " I ne'er admitted Love a guest
> In all the habitudes of life,"

had been brutalised and coarsened by the passage
of years into a loathing which finds its expression
in a horrified and disgusting flow of contempt
and sordid detail. In this poem one finds the
typical attitude, but it somehow lacks the urgency
of hatred which we should expect from Swift's
pen. Apart from the last eighteen lines, which
have the genuine ring, the verses are a little
pedestrian and perhaps read as slightly insincere
—as if we were reading a competent imitator.

Of the definite theme of the poem—" that love
is nothing else but pride "; that matrimony is
based on self interest—we may say that it is
quite in character with Swift's opinion. Again
we go to his *Thoughts on Various Subjects*, and
find " That the cause of most actions, good or
bad, may be resolved into the love of ourselves."
Furthermore his picture of the fashionable bride
whose mind is a chaos—

" Of Dress and Equipage and Drums,
  And Servants silver-liv'ried o'er,
  And fifty Thousand Follies more,"

is in line with his expressed opinions of the
wives of the wealthy—

" Bred a fondling and an heiress;
  Drest like any lady mayoress;
  Cockered by the servants round,
  Was too good to touch the ground;
  Thought the life of every lady
  Should be one continued play-day;
  Balls and masquerades and shows,
  Visits, plays and powdered beaux."

To sum up. The poem is definitely attributed
to Swift. The thought of this poem recalls the
Dean closely, and there are correspondences in
idea and method which are decidedly Swiftian.
Again, its apparent origin from a publishing
house with a great Swift tradition supports its
claim to authenticity. We have then a *prima facie*
case for genuineness. But from the point of view
of style there are some doubts. The personal
touch is lacking and so is the forceful vehemence
we might have expected. Again, something of
Swift's crisp definiteness of style is missing. No
writer lived up to his own definition of style as
" Proper words in proper places " more compe-

tently than Swift. Everything he wrote is crystal clear at the first reading. Here we feel that there is a tendency to drag, a hint that the form is hampering the writer in a manner alien to Swift's genius. Our opinion—and it is given subject to correction—is that it may well be a good imitation, though the external evidence is strong in favour of authenticity.

MARTHA WHITEWAY: SWIFT'S LAST FRIEND

A FEW years ago a neighbour knocked at the door of the writer's remote country rectory and handed in a small, flat, mysterious parcel. The contents proved to be a half sheet of black-edged notepaper, inscribed with the familiar crabbed handwriting of Swift, signed by the Dean, and witnessed by the Cathedral verger!

This unexpected document was an agreement made by the Dean with his cousin, Mrs. Whiteway, promising to pay one hundred pounds apprenticeship fee for her son John, " whenever he becomes to some able Chirurgian a Prentice . . . . for teaching him the Art of Chirurgery," dated May 1736.

A duplicate of this letter exists. It is an interesting example of the survival powers of Swift autographs. One half in London; the other half hidden in a County Tipperary farmhouse until the twentieth century; and both combining to tell of the beginnings of the career of a distinguished Dublin surgeon, John Whiteway!

This young man was grandson of Adam Swift, one of the six of the Swift brothers who sought their fortune in Ireland in the seventeenth century. The Dean did not live to have the satisfaction of seeing his *protégé* succeed. (Rather sad, this, because so many of the folk Swift assisted proved worthless). But succeed John Whiteway did, and he justified Swift's gift and later legacy. He became himself an "Able Chirurgian," officially attached to St. Patrick's Hospital, the Bluecoat School, and to Steeven's (founded, according to unreliable tradition, by the pig-faced Madam Steeven!) Moreover, he was one of the petitioners when the Royal College of Surgeons received its charter in 1784, and two years later he was elected the second president.

All this is rather bald information. But happily, that incredible versifying Doctor, John Gilbourne, adds a little humanity to Whiteway's portrait. In 1775 Gilbourne published a little book of most entertainingly doggrellish medical biography, with the grandiose title, *The Medical Review: a Poem; being a Panegyric on the Faculty of Dublin—Physicians, Surgeons and Apothecaries, marching in Procession to the Temple of Fame.*" It is an extraordinarily funny work, and it is highly improbable that any Irish poet ever achieved such triumphant bathos as :

" The fractur'd Skull, to Samuel Croker-King,
The broken Limb, Wounds and Luxations
bring;
There's no Disaster but he can set right,
With Splints, Trepan, and Bandage not too
tight."

His verses on Whiteway picture a prosperous,
kindly, business-like surgeon in the best tradition,
fashionable but charitable :

" Whiteway does many hospitals attend—
Orphans a father, the distressed a friend,
Soon find in him—heals all chirurgic ills,
And with well-gotten coin his coffer fills."

It is not altogether surprising that John Whiteway turned out to be a successful doctor, for his
mother, Martha Whiteway, the faithful friend of
Swift's years of decay, was an enthusiastic and
indefatigable amateur medico. Time and again
her letters to Swift are filled with enquiries about
ailments and advice about cures. " Be pleased
to answer," she demands, in 1735, " how does
your Leg do ? How is your Head ? How is
your stomach ? " A week later her anxiety
about Swift's bad leg overflows into a highly
technical epistle. " Your Shin gives me infinite
trouble. . . . I hope to God you have taken care
of it. If it is a running sore, dress it twice a day

with Venice turpentine and the yolk of an egg beaten together, an equal quantity of each. Spread it thick on a cloth and bathe it once a day in warm milk; if it is black and painful, apply warm rum to it often." As an afterthought she provides a prescription for Sheridan, the Dean's Cavan host. The amiable schoolmaster has been suffering from asthma, and Mrs. Whiteway has a remedy for that as well. "Drink warm ptisan and nothing else, except liquorice tea in the morning, and ride every day."

Sagacious Martha Whiteway! She had the satisfaction of hearing a fortnight later that the garrison doctor of Cavan had been giving the Dean the very treatment that she had prescribed, and that all was well!

Her affection and care for the neurotic, diseased, old man is touching, and she does deserve to be remembered warmly for her faithfulness to him. In the fire of criss-cross allegations volleyed at one another by Swift's biographers, Mrs. Whiteway has been accused of double dealing, but not one single word can be found in her correspondence to show anything but affectionate loyalty. When few were left who could endure the Struldbrug's savagery, she remained his friend. In one of his tragic, half-coherent letters of 1737, he says: "My friends have all forsaken me, except Mrs. Whiteway, who preserves some pity for my condition, and a few others who love wine that costs them nothing." Her " strong, high, tenor voice " was one of the last sounds he could hear. " Mrs. Whiteway has almost got into a consumption by bawling in my ears," he writes—one of his closing pathetic feeble jests. She was the last human he recognised, and when he could no longer bear even her presence she came secretly every few days to the Deanery to see that he was cared for properly.

Yes—Cousin Martha was a true friend. It is not fair to stigmatise her affection as cupboard love. For years the world knew that Swift had

> . . . . left what little wealth he had
> To build a home for fools and mad.

There were few prospects for her in that direction. She had nothing more to gain once Swift had been certified as incapable of managing his affairs. Her small legacy could not now be revoked. She might well have deserted him like the others. But in the midst of personal troubles and ill-health she preferred to stay by him; to guard his interests and to face the slanders of Pope and Orrery. One is glad that Swift came to lean on her during those last ten nightmare years, writing : " I have very few friends in want. I have kindred enough, but not a grain of merit among them, except one female, who is the only cousin I suffer to see me." Her final indignant protest against Swift's hole and corner midnight burial does her honour, with its offer to pay out of her own pocket for a few funeral decencies.

She writes to one of the executors thus:

" The indignation which the town have expressed at the manner of burying their Patriot, is a proof his memory is dear as his life was once so to them. . . . I appeal to yourself, whether ever you knew a gentleman whose corpse was not in danger of being arrested for debt, treated in such a manner—an executed criminal to whom the law doth not allow Christian burial could only be used thus by some slight acquaintance.

" Surely to hang the room Dr. Swift lies in with black, to give him a hearse and a few mourning coaches, would be judged a funeral sufficiently private for so great a man, and that he himself thought decency requisite at a funeral may be known by what he did for his honest trusty servant, Alexander McGee. If this expense be thought too much to be taken from the noble charity he hath bequeathed, I make the offer of doing it, and desire it may be taken out of my legacy, as the last respect I can pay to my great and worthy friend. If this favour be denied me, I shall let whoever mentions this affair in my hearing, know the offer I have made."

Her anger does credit to her loyalty and friendship.

INDEX